LIVING FREE!

40th ANNIVERSARY EDITION

LIVING FREE!

The Ultimate Guide to Self-Confidence and Personal Power

BOB TRASK

& MEDIA

MEDIA

Published 2022 by Gildan Media LLC
aka G&D Media
www.GandDmedia.com

Front cover design by David Rheinhardt of Pyrographx

Interior design by Meghan Day Healey of Story Horse, LLC

Library of Congress Cataloging-in-Publication Data is available upon request

ISBN: 978-1-7225-0510-3

10   9   8   7   6   5   4   3   2   1

This book is dedicated to Mom
for making me possible

CONTENTS

CHAPTER ONE

Life is an adventure, the rewards are feelings. Feelings are the highest altar of our consciousness.

CHAPTER TWO

The truth is surprisingly simple. We are all governed by Superconscious, conscious and subconscious functions. How do they work? How can we understand who we are, and how can our subconscious minds be used to guarantee success in any venture?

CHAPTER THREE

How to surrender to those things in life that plague you and by so doing eliminate their power to affect you.

CHAPTER FOUR

The words and concepts of Truth, Honesty, Belief, Fact, Opinion, Right and Wrong are defined in such a way as to clarify attitudes about reality. Real success is not possible without this clarity.

CHAPTER FIVE

This ARAS philosophy can help you be the most loved and loving person possible and thereby the most successful.

CHAPTER SIX

This deadliest and most widely spread disease will ruin our lives and the lives of our children if we don't stop it now.

CHAPTER SEVEN

How do you know when to take risks, when to rest? How can you get out of boredom, emotional paralysis or guilt? This simple diagram demonstrates a progressive understanding of how to win in all situations every time.

INTRODUCTION

Today, increasing numbers of people keep *Living Free* as their guide to lives of meaning and purpose. I am grateful to the many who have reached me with their wonderful stories. My deep thanks also to G&D Media for recognizing this growing movement and publishing this 40th anniversary edition.

As natural children of this Universe, we fully deserve to live in grace, to be blessed each day with the delights of life. I originally composed *Living Free* as a guidebook for my students who wanted to free themselves from the toxins of self-blame, self-doubt, and unworthiness. It worked for them and still works for many thousands of readers.

In these pages, you will find that, although freedom is our birthright—the internal aching of unforgiven self-shame and self-blame erode and weaken our ability to live free and confident lives. While healthy remorse is appropriate because it heals with time, guilt becomes a black mold in the soul and demands we be small and insignificant. As you move through each chapter of this book, may you discover how to disarm those voices and regain the freedom to be truly you.

My friend, there is a power in goodness and a power in love. We know that Light is greater than darkness—every sunrise proves that. There is a sunrise of goodness and love awakening in our human family now, and because these two are forces of nature, they are invincible. I am honored to know that Living Free has become a handbook for that awakening, proving that innocence and creativity are our natures. I feel confident today that you will find your life and your joy enhanced by the gifts of Living Free.

Bob Trask

2022

FOREWORD

Here is a simple, straightforward book that can change your life forever.

When I read this book, I experienced Bob Trask as a loving, courageous man with a real commitment to honesty.

He shares his insights and directs us towards practical ways to apply them in our own lives; and by sharing stories from his own life, he makes these insights real, gives them flesh and bones.

I have great confidence in the value that can be obtained by reading this book in an open, interested frame of mind.

If you want to give yourself the opportunity to be more of who you really are, you have come to the right place, and the right person.

Have fun!

Paul Williams
Author of *Das Energi*
June 1983

TO MY READERS

Since this book was first published under the title *The ARAS Guide to Conscious Living* and through the second printing entitled *A Look at Living Free*, I have watched its effect on people from all walks of life and from many nations.

I have received hundreds of letters from readers saying that this book renewed their lives, their marriages and their careers. Many of today's most successful business leaders say that it is responsible for their prosperity. There are no words to adequately express how thrilled I am with its success, and I have been warmly pleased by your letters. You have shown the courage and the self-love to not only read this book but to stick with its teachings through those periods of change which I know are sometimes difficult. For your courage and your ongoing success I offer you my thanks and my congratulations.

Bob Trask

Bellevue, Washington

January, 1987

CHAPTER ONE

Feelings

When I was a kid the world was a wonder to me. I knelt in the wet grass watching the colors of light shining through dew drops. I lay on grassy hillsides watching clouds blow across blue skies. Sometimes a redtailed hawk did lazy circles above me. My fascination was physical as well as mental. I felt my whole body thrilling and discovered a kind of mystical connection between myself and the wind that carried the hawk and clouds.

Rivers and oceans are like the wind: turning, flowing, breathing, living. All living things are in motion. The crashing surf along the coast and the towering thunder clouds over the desert rim fascinate and thrill me because they echo and reflect the life moving within me.

Things I feel most important to communicate are things I cannot communicate with words. They are larger than our language. They are feelings of urgency and feelings of delight.

When I was seven or eight years old I loved marbles. My marbles were my personal friends. I had tiny purees of red and blue and green that we called pee wees. Even as I'm telling you this I am remembering the way the light came through them, pouring their colors into me, transforming me, opening me up like a parachute and making me sing inside. Other marbles, not as tiny as pee wees, were normal shooting marbles. They were made of agate or glass that looked like agate. They were breathtaking reds, yellows, whites and blues all splashed together. They touched a part of me until I felt myself melting and at the same time singing.

I remember hearing somewhere that when Handel wrote the *Hallelujah Chorus* he wrote without a piano just as he heard it in his head, and that he was weeping for sheer joy at what he was hearing. Strange as it may seem, that is how a sack of marbles can make me feel.

When I was on an ambulance crew in San Francisco I once picked up a Chinese woman who had tried to commit suicide. After we had been driving around for about an hour from hospital to hospital trying to get someone to take her, we realized no one wanted her because they were not equipped for suicidal patients. She was forty-five years old but looked like she was thirteen. Her skin was flawless. She had a child-like simplicity and beauty. Every time I asked her why she wanted to die, what her problems could be that she would not want to live, she would look at me and scream, "Liar!" When I finally left her in the San Francisco General Hospital Emergency Room, she was tied to her gurney looking after me as I walked away. With hatred in her eyes, she was screaming, "Liar! Liar!"

I think now I recognize the lie she had caught me in. She was calling all of us important adult persons of the world liars. She could see that we had lost the truth. The world is made of beauty and simplicity. The patterns of light and love everywhere around us are visible and tangible only to children. When we forget that we are children we forget that everything we need for a full harmonious life is supplied. Then we begin to manipulate the world around us, making up tricks and methods and techniques to force the world around us into giving us things that we do not deserve. When I say deserve I do not mean earn. Children do not earn their beauty and their laughter and their happiness, but they deserve it because they are still perfect pure creatures of a perfect pure universe. Only when we grow older and become frightened by our guilt do we begin to mistrust the world around us and lose our innocence and understanding, the keys to happiness. The other day I heard an old Perry Como song in which he sings of childhood, ". . . once you leave its borders you may never return again." I'm betting that we can return again. What it will take for each of us is courage. We can share our journey back to that holy place with others, but we must each have the solitary courage to propel ourselves. It is my opinion that if we don't return, we must give up the world with all of its kites and marbles and clouds and hawks and children because they will remain outside our scope of appreciation, and are thereby things that we do not deserve.

How do you feel about that? Do you want to recapture that kind of joy and glow of childhood or are you so busily working on trying to be an adult that you have forgotten adulthood is only a game, a charade?

This book is about power—not nuclear power nor hydraulic power nor horsepower, but a power greater than any of those: personal power, the power that emanates from the vibrating core of your being, power that allows you not only to see the majesty of your dreams but to accomplish them and move on to even greater dreams. What it will require is courage.

In my years of working with people, I have learned that feelings are the basis for all other human endeavors. Feelings are the highest altar of consciousness.

All theological concepts and all curricula for greater understanding of people and how they function eventually boil down to a common foundation: *Feelings*. How people feel is the basis for all other human endeavors.

The leaders of tomorrow's world will not be people who live in their intellects, having lost their ability to laugh and play as children. Those people won't be listened to by the future generations. Leaders who serve that new wave of humanity will be people who always remember they are children in the process of developing their personal powers, their ability to feel color and music, and their ability to touch one another's hearts. The people who will run the universe into which this generation is moving will be the children.

The proceeding chapters of this book are designed to guide you through a pattern of self awakening, or self remembrance. Take each of these chapters, read it until you understand it and apply the principles so that you feel your life actually changing and your attitudes about yourself and your world changing. By the time you have finished this book, I hope you will have begun to recognize your true magnificence and to have a positive sense of excitement about your future.

CHAPTER TWO

Who Are You and What Are You Doing Here?

What are you doing here? What are you doing on this planet? What is the cause of your existing here at this time? What purpose do you have? Centuries of philosophers and religious thinkers have sought the answer. Each time they thought they had the answer they incorporated it into an organization or religion around which people flocked to feel security. Nothing intensifies the sense of insecurity as strongly as the sense of being temporary, a cosmic accident that will sputter out one day, after which you will be forever gone. For most of us it is devastating to think of not being part of an eternal pattern but rather being temporary happenstance in the chain reaction of an exploding universe.

So here is yet another philosophy for you, one that encompasses most of the others and yet stands on its own. Perhaps it will ring the bell of truth within you.

YOUR PURPOSE IN BEING HERE IS TO HAVE FUN EXPERIENCING AND EXPRESSING YOURSELF AND THEREBY GROWING. You have always lived and will always live. There is no beginning and no end to your life. Your life is not merely this existence on planet earth but an everlasting and continuing life that goes on eternally. During your eternal life you decided to manifest one part of you into physical form. Why would a pure and a perfect spirit want to manifest itself into a human form, especially in this "vale of tears?"

Imagine yourself for a moment as spirit, floating around in darkness; doing nothing, just *being*. You will quickly recognize that a spirit without opportunities to express itself is very much like a painter without canvas, a carpenter with no tools or wood, a teacher without students. You are a perfect and eternally living being with only two basic needs: To *express* and *experience* your Self.

There are three interesting facets of your consciousness: the conscious, subconscious and superconscious.

Conscious describes your limited awareness of "what is." The phrase "expanding your consciousness" simply means expanding your awareness. A man standing in the center of a valley, for instance, who is aware of the entire universe which surrounds him all at one time, including trees, rock, outcroppings, meadows, wildflowers, bees, birds, clouds, sky and river is more conscious than the boy standing beside him who is only aware of the itch on his nose and the stream at his feet. The man has expanded his consciousness beyond that of the boy. The path to the superconscious or Godself through this level lies through disciplining, which demands we *be here now.*

Subconscious is best described as a memory bank where all experiences of this lifetime are stored. Your belief system is the outgrowth of this system and most of your reactions to life are a result of that belief system.

Superconscious describes the awareness of your eternal SELF, encompassing all things visible and invisible, throughout eternity.

That these are three active states of cognition is only part of their story. Possessed within these states of awareness are powerful, creative forces which manifest each new step of one's reality. Putting it more simply, that which we perceive to be the reality around us is created by us each day. Everything that happens to us happens because we created its happening, even though many of the things happening to us are not what we would consciously choose. On some level we have decided to create such situations so that we may experience and express ourselves through them.

Your Subconscious Belief System:

Let's take a look at the mechanism by which you make subconscious decisions about your daily life. As mentioned earlier, your subconscious mind is a memory bank of experiences. You arrive fresh and new on this planet and immediately, on becoming aware of being here, begin having experiences and expressing yourself. Each experience is indelibly printed in your subconsciousness mind and almost immediately affects the way you *express* yourself. Notice how those stored experiences are the platform for expression—expression which becomes limited or advanced as a result of new experiences. (Every experience, without exception, is stored and may be recalled through regressive hypnosis or other methods.) So you see that you are here to experience and express your natural Self.

Your expressions are enriched by or soured by the wealth of your experiences thus far in life. An event may have taken place in your past that causes you to mistrust bald men with mustaches or feel most comfortable around the smell of popcorn. Thus, past experiences are always deciding not only your expressions, but your new experiences as well. You have stored countless millions of memories of experiences. Experiences multiply as you get older because each new experience affects dozens of old memories in such a way that they become re-experiences, more new experiences.

Memories can be powerfully destructive to your ability to lead a happy and productive life. What causes this phenomenon? We humans make complex and far reaching judgments about everything that happens to us. We decide that each experience is either better than or worse than, more than or less than something else. The result is that each time we have an experience (see Figure opposite), that experience is stored and encased within a judgment of itself. The experience loses its ability to be a multi-faceted learning experience. It becomes an experience that happens only as we judge it. You may have, for instance, finished second in a very difficult race. Your judgment about the race is that you lost because you did not come in first. Memories of the race then are of its being a failure on your part. Yet, another person who remembers finishing second may recall the race with excitement, knowing he won second place. The first person has a belief springing from his memory-bank subconscious that he has to win first place in order to be happy. The second has a belief that says winning second would be fantastic.

Your judgments, therefore, make the decision about how your subconscious mind stores the experience. Animals do the same thing, but with less complication. A coyote that has been caught in a trap becomes very clever at avoiding traps. Dogs are taught by punishment or reward. Even fish seem to store the memories of being attacked or hurt by other fish or larger animals, as well as where to find food under varied conditions.

You and I, because of our more complex ability to reason, store our memories relative to our survival as they relate to acceptance in our society. Quite often the judgments we make of those experiences are mistakes.

There was, for instance, in my grade school, a girl we called, "Bird Legs." She was an awkward girl, very tall, and had legs like broom-

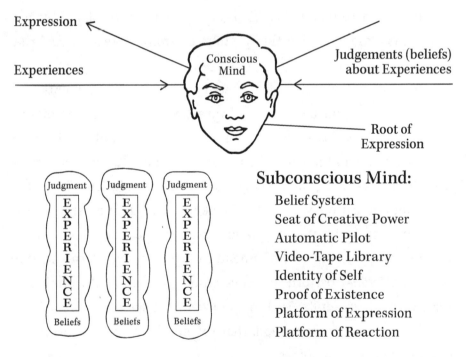

Expression

Experiences

Conscious Mind

Judgements (beliefs) about Experiences

Root of Expression

Subconscious Mind:

Belief System
Seat of Creative Power
Automatic Pilot
Video-Tape Library
Identity of Self
Proof of Existence
Platform of Expression
Platform of Reaction

Judgment — EXPERIENCE — Beliefs

Judgment — EXPERIENCE — Beliefs

Judgment — EXPERIENCE — Beliefs

Experiencing is the first step of Learning. There are hundreds of millions of experiences stored in the subconscious. The second step is the expression of that experience. It is impossible to express and experience without being influenced by the judgments and beliefs that surround it. When an experience is buried and one refuses to express its impact because of judgments held, it becomes a block. Thereafter, experiences and expressions relative to that block are charged with defensive behavior.

sticks. A few years later I returned to the same town to attend high school. I met her again. I could not believe my eyes! She was, by far, the most beautiful girl in the school, and her legs were so lovely it still makes me a little giddy just to think about it.

Was she, then, laughing and gay and excited about her beauty? No, she was not. Her subconscious program insisted she was awkward and had bird legs in spite of much evidence to the contrary. Her belief system told her to stay in the shadows like an ugly duckling. The flame of her self expression was all but smothered.

Each of us has our own "bird legs" story. Each one of us has stored in our subconscious minds billions of experiences so colored by our erroneous judgments that they prohibit us from expressing our true selves.

Because of my early life experiences and the judgments my superiors put upon me, I have always been considered by others and myself an oddball. As a child, I was judged by adults to be lazy, untrustworthy and much too arrogant. As an adult, I now see children of that same age and recognize that, by comparison, I was far more ambitious (today it's called "hyperactive,") than most of them. The labels of "untrustworthy" and "arrogant" resulted from: number one, my spending a lot of time in thought and wonderment; and second, a defense pattern that covered up the pain I felt from being rejected by most adults. My thoughts were not spoken because I felt they would not be understood, that I would be ridiculed. Silence is often mistaken for aloofness.

I was convinced that there was something wrong with me, that I could never fit in, never be a part, and since I had no father, no man would love me. The effect on my life from this early programming was devastating. Fortunately for me I had a powerful and wise mother who championed many of those things that others criticized. She knew I was different, but she saw that as a specialness. Even though we were poor and lacked the opportunities I might otherwise have had, she never failed to encourage me to fulfill my dreams. (Strangely enough, our poverty turned out to be a blessing. If we had been able to afford schooling for me I would no doubt have become a doctor or lawyer instead of working to support the family. I would not have had the opportunity for the wonderful education I received from the street teachers.) If it had not been for Mama's positive programming, I would never have had the courage to make it this far.

When I was a child I loved to sing. My voice developed early in life. For me, the experience of singing is the same experience I imagine a graceful hawk has flying on the summer wind. These soarings, however, were usually cut short by the voice of one of my elders telling me to pipe down or get far enough away so I wouldn't bother anyone.

Their main concern was not my singing. Their main concern was that I was developing at too early an age a love of my ability to sing, which, like the budding love of my own ability to think, was making me dangerously uncontrollable. They redoubled their efforts and were determined to see to it that I was a good and humble Catholic boy who did not try to best his elders.

Take a moment now and see how this fits with you and your life. Did you have natural talents or natural thought patterns and feelings that did not fit well with your parents and other authorities? Were you criticized for having those talents and did you learn then that the best thing for you was to go inside yourself?

You must be allowed to express yourself. Self expression is the only way to clear the self for new and larger experiences. Until expressed, experiences are unorganized images and feelings, ingredients for a new recipe never yet cooked, parts for a new machine not yet invented, notes to a song not yet written. The true expansion of self only takes place when experiences are transformed into expressions and given away for others to experience. We are each as individual as snowflakes. No two of us are exactly alike. Your expression, when honestly given, is unlike anything anyone else has ever experienced. When you allow the perfect form of your expression to be distorted by society's demand for conformity, you and society lose the one opportunity in eternity to behold an individual expression of Self.

In my particular situation, I could not deny my love for singing, nor could I pretend that my mind would quietly lie down and die. So I kept singing, and I kept dreaming, and I kept planning to be a great man leading others through great adventures.

My voice developed and filled out and my singing was exciting. I sang the sweet old songs of Perry Como and Nat King Cole, the passionate songs of work and love from Harry Belafonte's collection, and wrote and sang my own as well. The early years of adverse programming had not affected my voice; however, serious damage had been done to my self esteem and self confidence. I sang more out of an attitude of, "I'll show you," than an attitude of, "I know you are loving my song." The defensiveness made the subtle songs devoid of passion, while the fiery songs of rebellion made the listener feel he was being attacked. Whenever I began to sing, I always felt a sense of urgency, a sense of fear crowding and pushing me. I consequently found myself rushing the music and breaking meter. When working with a band or orchestra, I felt dominated by the musicians. I remember a show at the Stardust Hotel in Las Vegas. The musicians were a "pick-up" band, one made up of musicians from the local union. They included musicians from the great bands of Woody Herman, Roger Miller, and Sammy Davis Jr. My confidence was gone. I was once again a child amidst stern and capable elders who would surely not like my singing. I felt that I was secretly criticized. I lost the meter and talked too much.

Thanks to the superiority of the players who never once showed any open disapproval and who played marvelously, and thanks to the fact that I did "get into" most of the songs, we still got standing ovations. It is important to note here that not only did none of my family see the Stardust show, they never saw any show I did for the seven years I struggled as a singer and actor. Their absence validated my feeling of unworthiness.

For each of those seven years, I struggled and starved and had sporadic success as an actor-singer. Deep inside of me was the nagging conviction that I could never make it because I was really just a smart aleck kid trying to show off his voice that no one wanted to hear.

There is a pattern here you might recognize, a pattern by which you might see the causes and purposes for some of your own failings. I was told I was great by many of the most knowledgeable people in show business, not the least of whom was Elton Rule, President of the American Broadcasting Corporation. Mr. Rule went to great lengths to help me establish my career. Each time an important appointment or audition was arranged for me, I would sabotage it. I did not consciously know that I was sabotaging it, but the subconscious pattern was set. I was convinced by my early programming that I was a failure and could not, no matter how hard I tried, ignore the subconscious conviction. It seemed more powerful than my conscious mind and more powerful than my will power. The programs and the tapes of your subconscious mind are in fact the identity of you that is stamped in your mind. When you attempt to override your subconscious, you feel you are a phony pretending to be something you are not. Others read your efforts as pretense and label you a phony in their minds.

After seven years in show business—with a few bit parts in motion pictures and TV commercials, and a few real wins as a singer, I gave up. Giving up was the most difficult thing I had ever done. I was admitting at last that my sentence to being a failure was absolute and there was nothing I could do about it.

My life had been a constant battle of contradictions. I had the ability and yearning to sing, dance, act, and perform well as an athlete. I could organize courses, teach, speak and inspire thousands of people. I knew this was true because I did all of it and more. Yet, I was always plagued by the sickening knowledge that I was not worthy of success, really a failure, a smart alecky kid pretending to more than he was. No less than seven times in my life, I have created business enterprises which involved vast fortunes and limitless approval for myself. Each time, I sabotaged and destroyed the entire enterprise at the very peak of its success. Does this sound familiar to you? My identity of myself, which was set up and programmed into me at a very early age, said that I could not have those successes, that I did not deserve all that approval and that I had no right to be rich. The pattern further stated that if I did manage to attain those things it would be through "conning" others and I would eventually have to pay a great penalty to atone for it.

Unworthiness will always produce failure. Several years ago, I wrote *Tulip*, a book on first aid emergency rescue which has since been used by colleges and agencies across the country. Very few people even know I wrote the book. I did not have it published myself, nor did I copyright any of the information. I didn't feel worthy. Do you have a book lying on a shelf somewhere that has never quite gotten to the publishers? Do you have a yen to express yourself creatively in some way and have never dared? Or have you, like myself, accomplished many works of your own perfect expression and yet could not accept the win?

The way subconscious programming works is as follows: Each time an event occurs, your experience of it is altered so that it fits with your subconscious filters. In my case, for instance, at a young age I was programmed by myself and others to a certain way of thinking about *me*. Experiences that came about in later life were constantly altered so they would fit with my overall subconscious identification of self. Thus, the idea of having a gold record, of being delivered to Carnegie Hall in a chauffeur-driven limousine, of being able to turn on my car radio and hear my own voice, or of being successful in any of my other enterprises was in absolute contradiction to the overall subconscious attitude of who I was. Even though I was desperately and doggedly attempting to succeed, subconsciously I undermined and sabotaged every step I made. It might also be noticed at this point that I blamed everyone in my universe for these failures except myself.

Part of my purpose in creating this book and ARAS Trainings is to share with you the techniques and methods of deprogramming early deteriorative conditioning that have worked for me. Proof that these reconditioning and reprogramming techniques work is the book you are now reading.

I would like to mention here that all my subconscious programming was not deteriorative, otherwise I would not have had the principles and sense of integrity necessary to be saying these things. So the good news is that subconscious programming can be made to serve you as easily as it has been used to hinder you. Some of the things my elders programmed into me that serve me well are: always stand up to fear the first time it appears; go to the mountains for lessons in peace and to the sea for lessons in surrender; you can't catch a fish unless your line is in the water; tearing a thing down takes exactly 1/100 of the effort to build it; you can't lose that which is yours; everyone either rents or borrows, no one owns; the top of the mountain is just over the next ridge; what goes around comes around; give the urgent job to the busiest person; fish bite the bait that looks like it's getting away; a horse doesn't know how to buck until he's ridden; if you are giving someone a push make sure they are out of gear; no one can love you more than you love you; all pain comes from resistance; solutions are 180 degrees from problems; when you are studying the problem the solution is behind you.

Every business is the "People Business"; sales people are the world's teachers; the reason politicians change after being elected is because we expect them to; there is only one religion; the scaredest person is the fiercest fighter; the angriest person is the easiest to beat; people with easy paths are walking downhill; people who really know don't teach; there is more vital information in a rose petal than a college; birds don't have police (they'll get mugged one of these days); most solutions create bigger problems; what you resist persists; angels fly because they take themselves lightly; we are going, back to the sea; chili is best on hotcakes; what I can perceive I can achieve; non-gamblers never win; ruts are premature graves—expectations are premature resentments; possession is a barrier to communication; death is birth; God is a grasshopper; ducklings learn to waddle by walking behind their mother; learning is experiencing; experiencing is receiving; teaching is expressing; expressing is giving; giving is receiving; now is forever; tomorrow is an illusion; children know until they are dismembered; adults try to remember themselves; disease is dis-*ease*; to pray to God is the path, to pray with God is the goal; the path and the goal are God; it is the way it is; the way it is, is the way it is.

Several years ago, a British physicist was asked to draw the schematic for a computer that would equate the power and retention capacity of a human subconscious mind. His report back was that it would require a package no smaller than the Empire State Building to house such a computer. Remember! He was talking about the capacity of your mind. I think now in the age of printed circuits that is no longer true. Nonetheless, those proportions were impressive. Fantasize just for a moment yourself standing on the street in New York looking up at the Empire State Building. While imagining that, also imagine all of your creative capacity, all of your subconscious power and the library of all you have learned and know are housed in that building. The Empire State Building is filled completely to capacity with your mind and there is no room left over. If you will learn to acknowledge the creative power you are housing, there will be no thing you cannot do. If the amount of energy used to sabotage your efforts becomes instead used for your benefit, the possibilities will be limitless.

In order for you to put the maximum charge of excitement, confidence and joy in your life, you must first decide a direction. Your life's joy is dependent upon your having goals, striving for them and accomplishing them.

Dare to dream. Visualize yourself being, doing and having that dream. It takes courage to dream of really winning big, but I guarantee that if you follow the precepts outlined here you will absolutely gain that which you seek. There is only one condition. These principles will only work when the dream is void of resentment and revenge. Dreams of destroying old enemies are not the dreams that will fulfill your life.

So visualize yourself *having already attained* that dream and then there are two things you can start doing right away. Number one is to dilute the undesirable beliefs of your subconscious by creating confidence, building wins in your life and recognizing them as you create them. Every day, whether you realize it or not, you win many times. Of course, the subconscious being programmed towards maintaining a humble image tries not to allow you to recognize them as wins. So a new attitude must begin to build, one in which you happily acknowledge each win you make no matter how small. Far from making you egotistical and superior, constant acknowledgment of yourself as a winner will make you calm and powerful.

The second technique for you to begin immediately is: In order to reprogram your belief system to serve you, create a powerful and positive affirmation and repeat it with deep conviction at least fifty times per day, and at each of those times when you are being plagued with self doubt. Such a positive affirmation is: "I am calm and I am powerful." This is an excellent positive affirmation for someone who is feeling weak and frightened or scattered and confused.

I will suggest more positive affirmations; however, your affirmations must be ones that fit your particular needs. To be most effective a positive affirmation should start with the words: "I am . . ." and should state quickly an simply the affirmation's objective. Do not use negatives, as negatives are not registered in the subconscious mind. It is like saying to a child, "Do not think of a brown cow." You have just created a brown cow where there was none before. An affirmation that says, "I am not fat," registers in the subconscious without the "not," i.e., "I am fat."

When these affirmations are repeated, they should be done with as much thought as possible given to the meaning of the words being said. Once embarked upon, they should be repeated no less than 25 times in the morning, soon after waking, and 25 times in the evening before going to sleep. Following this routine faithfully for one month will bring many wins you never dreamed of. Following it for two months will change your life.

Most affirmations will go through a set of stages when practiced daily. The first stage is disbelief. It is easy to quit here because the words, "just don't fit me." This stage usually lasts only a week but may last as long as a month. Do not give up! Keep affirming while *visualizing* yourself already being that which you affirm.

The second stage you will probably feel is disassociation, in which the affirmation seems to have no meaning; you neither believe nor disbelieve it. This is an easy time to quit. Most people quit right here. Don't give up! Your subconscious is letting go of its negative control. Keep it up and keep concentrating on your visualization. This stage may last a couple of weeks.

Stage three is the miracle stage. You will become aware that the affirmation is true and that you can do anything you want. This stage will begin in three to five weeks and will last as long as you want it to. Continue this affirmation at least two weeks after you enter this stage, and repeat it if ever you begin to relapse.

This may seem tedious and it may seem like a long time. Keep in mind, however, that you have a lifetime of negative programming to be undone in a relatively short period of time, and that the release of your powers of creation will be so exciting and will create such strides in your personal life that you will look back on these months of work as a very small investment for what you have gained.

A positive affirmation for someone who suffers from feeling trapped and duty bound in their life is, "I am free." When saying these words visualize yourself as free, soaring over the mountaintops, unencumbered by responsibility.

For those of you who would like to have more self confidence an affirmation might be: "I am truly a winner, winning more every day." While affirming bring to mind wins you have recently had. You should be able to count at least thirty wins for each day. If that is not possible it does not mean you are not having those wins; it means you are not recognizing them. Each of us in daily life has at least fifty wins. Examples of such wins are temptations you have overcome; times when you have been gracious when it would have been easy to have been otherwise; getting yourself busy to handle tasks when you would like to procrastinate; taking the time out to rest when you would rather go on; making it a point to "ARAS" someone special in your universe and so on.

All sickness and disease is produced by negative thinking and improper living. You can use the *reprogramming* methods described here to cure any ailment—physical, mental or emotional. It will take a little courage and perseverance, and *you can do it!*

Make your affirmation describe your wellness and visualize it being so. Begin today to use your subconscious power to make your life all it can be. Remove from your subconscious mind confidence blocks and destructive attitudes. Replace them with the positive knowledge that you are a winner and that starting right now *you are winning.*

CHAPTER THREE

It Is the Way It Is

Did you ever wonder how a swami in India could lie on a bed of nails and go to sleep? What must it be like to have all of those nails poking into the tender parts of your body? Don't you think the pain would be excruciating?

I once watched a man preparing to walk across a bed of hot coals. He sat down beside me on a low wall and we talked. The people gathering around us eyed him suspiciously. I looked at his feet. The soles were soft and pink. There was no protection from the heat.

I leaned over and said in a quiet voice, "Tell me the truth. How do you do it? How do you keep from burning your feet?"

He looked peaceful. "I don't resist the heat," he said softly. "It is the resistance that burns."

I did not know what he meant. Whether or not he resisted the heat, it seemed to me like his feet would burn up.

I was perplexed and curious. He got up and walked over to the beginning of a twenty foot long pit filled with white hot coals. I watched him closely, convinced that he would not be able to make the walk without burning himself unless he used some trick. I looked for the trick, the balm, ointment or perhaps false soles he might slip on at the last moment. I was no more than five feet away. I studied the pit for ash-colored rocks and areas that looked like coals onto which he might step. I watched him carefully. He centered himself, took a deep breath, and walked slowly forward. His feet would sometimes push through the surface into the deeper coals. I could feel the heat parching my skin from where I stood. There was no doubt about the heat of the coals. He walked with calm deliberate steps the full length of the pit, and when he reached the end everyone exhaled at once, clapping and cheering.

He walked back over and sat down beside me. "May I see your feet?" I asked. He allowed me to inspect both feet. I looked closely; they were not burned. They were dusty with ashes, but beneath the ashes were the same pink soled feet I had seen before he went into the fire.

"Doesn't it ever burn?" I asked.

"Oh yes," he replied. "Sometimes I can only walk a few feet. It depends on how much I am able to surrender."

The word "surrender" had been coming up in my life over and over again. Surrender to me had always meant "giving up." I prided myself in being one who would hang on till death. And yet my dogged stubbornness did not earn me anything except the pride in being stubborn. I was afraid that surrendering to anything would weaken my resolve and I would become an ineffectual person.

Since that day with the fire walker I have learned that surrender does not mean giving up or collapsing my dreams or admitting defeat. I have learned that the opposite is in fact true, that perfect surrender assures victory for me in all endeavors. The universe is flowing as a river flows in perfect ever-changing patterns on its way to the eternal sea from whence it comes. Imagine that you have jumped into this river of life from the end of a rickety old dock at the end of which a water-logged rope trails in the current. You decided to plunge into the river of life, took a deep breath, and jumped off the dock. But before you had gotten more than barely wet you changed your mind. It seemed too drastic, too frightening, so you grabbed at the nearest thing to you which happened to be the rope. You are now in the river of life, hanging on to your rope, going nowhere. The water is beating against you. Your arms are growing tired. Your hands are growing tired. Your greatest fear is that the rope might break or that you might accidentally slip and let go. The symbolic rope is that attachment you have to being "right." You are afraid if you let your beliefs go they would disappear and you would be left with nothing to validate your existence.

So I ask you, where would you be if you let go of the rope that is attached to your belief system? The truth is you would be in the river of life where you are anyway. The difference is, you would no longer be fighting the natural flow. You would be drifting with it.

You arms are now aching. Your sides are aching from breathing against the flow of the current. Surrendering means letting go of the rope. If you let go of the rope you will notice that the pain in your hands and arms and sides will go away. You can lie on your back and watch the sky. You can see the trees drift by and watch the children and animals playing by the banks of the river. You will be caressed and carried by the same current that once assaulted you. You will be free to swim where you please back and forth to either side and when you regain your strength, you will even be able to go back up the river a ways. Your life will now be surrendered to the flow of the river.

If at any time you become frightened, there will always be another rope trailing in the water for you to grab because ropes are important. It is necessary from time to time for you to resist the flow so that you can be impressed by its power and renewed in your conviction of surrender as a way of life.

Your life story has been one of alternating resistance and surrender. When you resist, you are in pain, and what you resist is always the natural flow of truth; the way it is.

You are a part of the river of life. Little by little throughout the eternity of your being you are surrendering and flowing with life as it is. As you surrender you find to your delight that you are not being tossed and jerked in wild, erratic directions; you are being smoothly fitted into the pattern of Mother Nature.

Surrendering allows your will and power to spring from the Light; the perfectly patterned flow of eternal life. And as a result you will now have the strength of the river's flow to support your dreams. Your power will be magnified many times.

How will you know when you are not flowing with the river, when you are resisting? A warning device sends messages through your system when you forget to surrender. The message is pain. The pain will frighten you and stir you to action. To make the pain go away find what you are resisting and surrender to it. Remember the firewalker's words, "It's the resistance that burns."

Are you working on a job you dislike? Are you doing daily work that is unsatisfactory and unfulfilling? If so, you are in physical, mental and emotional pain. The alarm is sounding: "Let go of the rope." Either change the parts of the job that you dislike or change careers. Find your own special work, begin it and the pain will go away.

Surrender! It is by dogged resistance to the natural flow of life that you force yourself day after day into a place where you do not belong. The false sense of security that you have in that job has deceived you into thinking you cannot do anything else. You read the growing list of unemployed people to lend validation to your fears. Keep in mind that unemployed people are people who are not working. Do not measure yourself by them. They have a completely different attitude than yours. You are working, and you can work for the rest of your life, for yourself, doing your own work if you would like to. Don't align yourself with people who have decided not to work.

Is it your relationship that is causing you distress? Is there spoken or unspoken resentment between you and a loved one? Each pain, physical, mental and emotional, can be traced back to a point of resistance. Remember this: *It is the way it is* and resistance does not alter it. Resistance only brings you pain. When you feel pain you are being reminded of your stubbornness and resistance to what is.

You may direct events differently in the future to avoid the thing which you now resist. However, the course of events at this moment is what it is.

The way it is, reality, which dictates the course of the river of life is usually ignored by us. We preoccupy ourselves instead with fantasies of how-it-should-be or how-it-could-be and fool ourselves into believing and trying to live those fantasies.

A major cause of disharmony in relationships is involvement with soap operas that dwell on marital instability. Housewives and husbands who get personally involved with these programs every afternoon can become so caught up in those drama situations that they experience them as real. Their mates, coming home from work in the evenings, sometimes find them in a condition of distress over a crushed love affair or marital tragedy that happened in a soap opera during the day. Some of these TV watchers relate to the fantasy situations depicted in programs to such a degree that real marriage relationships are undermined by those phantom situations. The other spouse having not seen the programs is usually at a loss as to how to act to restore harmony.

Whenever reality is ignored fantasy takes its place. The result is unrest and loss of real communication in relationships. Ultimately, the "real" situation begins to suffer and conform to the pressures of the fantasy so that eventually the fantasy will become real. This is basically the way in which we create our own reality.

There is an excellent story about a young man who goes off to college and falls madly in love with a beautiful girl he sees the first day of class. The girl is so lovely that he is afraid to approach her. Even though she sees him looking at her he never speaks a word. As the school year passes by she becomes an illusionary playmate of his. He knows her name; he knows where she lives; he even knows her phone number. He knows all of her friends. He knows which classes she is taking, where her parents live and what her father does for a living. In his fantasy, he sees himself someday being married to her. He dreams of taking her to the prom, he dreams of taking her fishing, he even dreams of taking her to bed. He dreams of taking her everywhere. But this relationship is carefully kept from being real. She is truly the girl of his *dreams*.

Eventually she goes out with and becomes pinned to a football player. In the mind of this young man the football player stole his girl. He might well have written the song, "On Top Of Old Smokey," which says, "I lost my true lover for courting too slow." If, in fact, she was his *true* lover then he was not courting too slow. If he was courting too slow then she, in fact, was not his *true* lover but rather a fantasy lover.

Fantasy/reality that surrounds our lives is truly amazing. When the cruel and cold realities of life seem too much for us, we, like a child hiding from the boogey man, have a warm electric blanket of illusions that we pull up over us; illusion fostered and fed by inane television programs, inane movies and inane music.

There are excellent television programs and movies and quite a bit of excellent music, but excellence is decidedly in the minority.

There is no pressure on television, movie or music producers to produce excellence. The audience is so hooked on fantasy they have become blind to art.

Pearl Buck in her book, *The Good Earth*, explores Karl Marx's theory of the "opium of the people." The opium she wrote about was that vehicle most commonly used to move peoples' awareness from a position of realizing the here and now into someplace more tolerable.

Only by accepting and flowing with *our own lives* can we begin to know who we really are as eternal selves. Creating fantasies amid the realities of life enables us to hide our true selves and thereby diminish the chance of experiencing and expressing our eternal selves. We will each make the discovery of our eternal identity only if our discovery processes are uncluttered by illusion or fantasy.

The first step in getting one's life in order is to admit to reality; *IT IS THE WAY IT IS*. Learn to stop worrying your mind about what might be next week and what happened last week. As I sit here in my kitchen writing this book, I see that the pen only writes where it touches the paper. You only experience your life where it presently is. The dried ink of the past does not represent who and what you now are. The future is yet to be written. Both past and the future are true fantasy—the future, in that it has not consciously happened to you yet, and the past, in that the moment after any incident happens your perception of it begins to be distorted by, current realities and your ever changing viewpoint. The past is never remembered exactly as it happened. Instead, it is viewed through what I call retroactive distortion—a distortion resulting from memory being subjected to the overwhelming pressures of beliefs. We normally do not travel back in time to recreate the scene as it originally was; we look back from our present viewpoint and see the way we *believe* it to have been. We are inspired by our dreams, motivated by our fears and either sabotaged or aided by our belief systems. Our beliefs wield incredible power. Our creative and destructive forces are guided by them. That is why it is so important to restructure our belief systems to be sure that they validate and support our perfection.

Let's do a simple exercise in reality/fantasy. Hold one hand a comfortable distance from your face and study it carefully. Examine the back, the finger print swirls, the veins, the callouses on the palm. Has it changed since you were a tiny child when you were fascinated by your hands and fingers and how they worked? Now, slowly bend and unbend your fingers. Move your hand in such a way that you are able to experience the amazing fluidity of motion that it possesses. Do not read further in this book until you have spent two full minutes in this exercise.

While you were studying your hand you were focused in reality, in the here and now. There is so much beauty slipping past you each moment of each day because your focus of attention is somewhere other than the present.

Fantasy has its place in our life. It is an excellent retreat when we need rest. Fantasy also guides our destiny in that we daydream and imagine in our fantasy world before we begin to physically create.

Quite often, though, we stay in the world of fantasies and imagination and never create anything except more fantasies. A fantasy world seems like a safe world to live in. It can, however, leave your real life empty and unfulfilled.

In the following chapter I would like to give you some of my definitions of reality. You may find in studying them that they jolt that fantasy of your thinking a bit. If they do, so much the better.

CHAPTER FOUR

In Search of Truth

1. Truth: What is (not provable)

Great thinkers have for hundreds of years been attempting to define truth. It has been defined as "what seems to be," as, "what you believe to be," and as, "honesty." I believe the best definition to be: Truth is *what is*. Your observation or my observation of a tall green cottonwood tree has no effect on the tree. It is of no importance if I call it a sycamore and you call it an oak. My seeing it as a sycamore and your thinking it an oak does not change the truth. It is still a tall, green cottonwood tree. The truth is *what is*—not what seems to be truth! But what is truth?

Sometimes, because of our fascination with fantasy we seem unable to get focused on truth. The search for truth is a task worthy of your time. Try to investigate these situations without letting your beliefs distort your perceptions: What is the truth about your relationships, about your job and about your health? If after a close look at the truth you find that these things are not the way you want them to be, what is the truth about what you can do about them? Jesus said, "Know the truth and the truth will set you free." Do you want to be free? Then be a seeker of truth. A seeker of *what is*.

There is no thing that is not. If you can see, perceive or sense a thing, then *it is*. Beyond that, many things *are* that we are not yet free enough to perceive. *There is no thing that is not.* If it is, in any way, then *it is*. Truth is what is. All things are true. There is no thing that is not true. We have misused the word "truth" to mean "accurate." A thing may be inaccurate or non-factual and still be true. Two and Two, for instance do not make five. That inaccuracy is not an untruth. If a child writes on his school paper, 2 + 2 = 5, at that moment if becomes truth—*what is*. It does not mean that two marbles plus two marbles equal five marbles. It means that on that child's paper, 2 + 2 = 5. There is no way of getting around that.

I remember a dear friend who I will allow to remain anonymous by calling "Fred." Fred played guitar for me when I worked as a singer. He smoked a lot of pot. Another friend accompanied me to Fred's house for a rehearsal one day. As we sat talking, Fred rolled a joint, lit it and passed it to me. In those days I believed marijuana to be just one step from heroin addiction so I passed the joint to my friend. His reaction was as though he'd been shocked. Not only did he not want a puff, he didn't want to touch or be involved with it in any way. His reaction confused Fred, "What's wrong, man? You look like something bit you."

My friend, shaken, stood up and stoutly declared, "I do not believe in marijuana." Fred at first appeared hurt; then he began to smile and was soon laughing. "What do you mean you don't believe in it?" he asked gaily. He was enjoying this.

"Just that," my friend's voice was tight, "I don't believe in marijuana."

Later after my friend had left Fred shook his head and smiled. "The guy said he doesn't believe in marijuana. Can you beat that?" he asked.

"But lots of people don't believe in marijuana," I said. "What's so strange about that?"

He pointed to a joint in the ashtray. "Can't you hear what you are saying, man? *It is.* Look at it. It is. How can you not believe in it? You can not like it or not smoke it, but how can you not believe in it? It is."

I have never forgotten that lesson about truth. All things are true. Whether you believe in them or not does not change them.

You'll notice below a 360 degree truth circle. This circle represents all of life; everything seen and unseen, experienced and unexperienced. Encompassed within this circle are all the experiences of and observations of all people. Also encompassed within the sphere are all things that have never been observed or experienced and perhaps

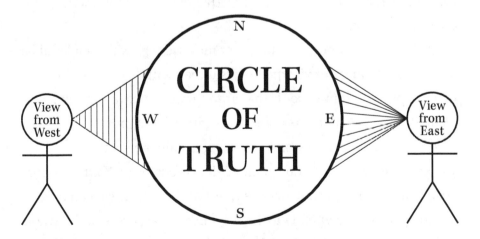

What if each of these characters were to realize that there is no thing that is not, that all things are true including his and his opponent's viewpoint? He could then double his grasp of truth.

never will be, for the ingredients of truth are limitless in number and variety.

Notice the two stick figures at each side each seeing his own viewpoint of truth. Notice also that from the viewpoint each has taken there is no more information possible. Both are seeing everything that their position allows. In order to see more or know more it is necessary for you to be willing to change your position.

Do you remember the old story about five wise men who were blindfolded and taken to experience an elephant? Each man was given an opportunity to touch and pat the animal; he was then taken inside a room with the others and the blindfolds were removed. Each man began to describe his experience of the elephant. One man said the elephant was very much like a tree for he had felt the great leg of the animal. Another man said the elephant was very much like a cliff for he had touched its massive side. Another man said the elephant was like a rope, he had felt the tail—and so on. The point is that each man had a different opinion about what an elephant is. Yet none of them individually nor all of them together could encompass the truth about an elephant.

My viewpoint and your viewpoint may seem provable and still be opposites. Because our viewpoints disagree we find ourselves in argument. A point to remember is that arguments are always intended to disqualify another person's point of view in order to protect your own. If you don't defend your point of view it usually needs no defending, you are convinced that your point of view is accurate. Your only purpose in arguing is to convince me that I am wrong. If we could learn to see opposing viewpoints as corresponding balancers of the whole pattern of truth we would be glad to hear the other's viewpoint.

Picture this example: I am standing on one side of a door. I call through the door to you and say, "It's black on this side." You call through the door from your side and say, "It's white on this side." We have both learned twice as much about the door as we had previously known. If, however, we both feel it important to defend our positions by obstinately refusing to accept the other person's facts as part of the truth, we curtail our ability to learn and drive away anyone holding a differing viewpoint.

Facts are easily proven and easily defended; whereas, truth cannot be proven because there is no objective parameter against which to measure it. (All things, including parameters, are part of truth.)

It is easy to prove that the air above us contains certain basic elements such as oxygen and hydrogen for these are facts. It is another matter to prove that the air above our heads is varying shades of blue which at times change to all the colors of the rainbow—this is truth.

2. Honesty: Being one with what is

"Being-one-with-what-is," is being one with the truth, blending with what is, surrendering to truth. It means being willing to acknowledge that *what is, is,* and that *it is the way it is.*

Being dishonest is labeled by our society as bad and wrong. You can, however, be dishonest by simply not recognizing truth. Unless we are mentally and emotionally "clean" enough to recognize truth and then to represent it accurately, without embellishments, we are dishonest. Dishonesty is representing other than *what is,* i.e., truth. Being dishonest means not being true to yourself and about yourself; not being one-with-what-is; not living according to *what is*; living in a fantasy state; living in a state other than *the way it is.* These are states of dishonesty that come about because we haven't the courage to look at reality. We pretend truth is what we want it to be instead of what is. We are all dishonest in as much as we have not surrendered to the Law of Nature and flow of truth.

There is another kind of dishonesty; deliberate dishonesty. A person who knows truth and deliberately represents it differently. This person is destroying his connection with his eternal Self for some temporary gain. Deliberate dishonesty is a crime against Self as well as against nature and causes erosion of one's self confidence and self image. Deliberate dishonesty is most dangerous. All destructive forces spring from it.

3. Beliefs: What my memory tells me is true

All beliefs relate to the past. They derive from that combination of experiences and judgments that are stored in your subconscious mind or "belief system." When you hold on to old beliefs you are ignoring the truth that springs from evidence and new experiences. Every new experience you have is cross referenced by your entire belief system. These beliefs change the shade, shape and meaning of all new experiences so they become consistent with old beliefs. Our ability then to perceive *what is* is limited by our previously established belief system. Therefore, in our pursuit to experience *truth* we must allow our belief systems to be as flexible as possible.

You are, each day of your life, surrounded by a universe filled with new patterns of light and new opportunities for unfoldment through your experiences. When you doggedly resist all except that which you previously perceived to be true, you exclude from your life all truths but the ones that form the tiny rope onto which you are holding.

You create your reality according to the concepts that you believe to be true. When, for instance, you believe yourself to be ill, you remain ill until your mind opens enough to see that illness is only a tiny part of your whole experience and that being healthy is also yours for the taking. *You will experience your life exactly the way you believe it to be.* Your belief system keeps your attention focused on it and denies that there are any truths beyond itself. However, your reality comes each day, the unlimited garden of life and light. You create by intending a thing to be, and your intention is directed by your attention. WHATEVER HAS YOUR ATTENTION ALSO HAS YOUR INTENTION AND THEREBY IS CREATED BY YOU EACH DAY.

A person who has what we call a "closed mind," is a person who does not allow new evidence to alter previously conceived beliefs. Such a person sees his identity and proof of his very existence evidenced only by old beliefs. The way he affirms his old beliefs is by creating and viewing situations in such a way that they only validate what he previously thought to be so.

Our subconscious minds are libraries of memories. They are, however, not passive libraries openly accepting new information. Your ego is the librarian of your subconscious; a librarian who refuses to admit any information into the library which does not agree with the philosophies of the first few books the library ever acquired. Those first books, (first memories) taught our ego a certain point of view and in so doing gave it a platform from which to view all new books (experiences). Our librarian either refuses to accept new books (experiences), or rips out pages and distorts them until they agree with those first books (beliefs).

4. Fact: One provable particle of truth

Fact is only one particle of truth. An important part of proving a fact is the elimination from your experiment of anything not pertinent to the isolated fact you seek to validate. In fact, most proof of this kind could be termed isolation rather than validation for the results are the same. For instance, to prove the point that gravity pulls matter toward the center of the earth we conduct an experiment limited to the measurement of gravitational force on a piece of matter. Excluded from our test is centrifugal force caused by the spinning of the earth on its axis and other facts that seem irrelevant. The fact we then prove is true, but it is not truth because truth encompasses all.

Truth, unlike fact, is not provable because the very experiment we use to prove truth is an important part of truth itself. We would be using truth to prove truth. It would be like asking a man to fill out an employment application and to write his own name in the part that calls for character references.

We have looked here at the differences between fact and truth. Fact is a small provable viewpoint of truth; truth is all encompassing, what is.

5. Opinion: My viewpoint of truth (provable by my belief system)

Facts are provable scientifically whereas opinions are reflections of our belief system. Most of us get stuck here. We use our belief system as validation for the opinion that we exist. We view the pillars of our belief system as a sailor views distant islands. We know where we are (here) by seeing where our islands (beliefs) are in relation to us. When the sailor leaves an island behind and sails over the horizon, he does so with the faith that being out of sight of landmarks does not mean being lost, but rather being free to explore new horizons. Let go of your tightly clutched opinion and be free to be the ever changing, born new each day person you are, instead of being mired in the identity dictated by your beliefs. Your mind, like a parachute, works best when it is open.

RIGHT: CONSISTENT WITH MY BELIEF SYSTEM

   —My opinion

WRONG: INCONSISTENT WITH MY BELIEF SYSTEM

   —My opinion

Must we always mentally decide how to feel about experiences? Can't we let experience take us where it will? The answer is usually no because each experience that happens is used by us to validate who we believe ourselves to be. If the experience invalidates who we believe ourselves to be we label it wrong. If we can view it in such a way that it does validate who we believe ourselves to be we will label it right.

On a conscious level our only proof to ourselves that we exist at all is through the collective storehouse of memory. If we lose touch with our memory banks we lose our identity. Loss of identity is terrifying because we only exist relative to our stored observations (beliefs).

Descartes said, "I think, therefore I am." The statement of those who allow their beliefs to control their lives might state: "I remember, therefore I am." If someone attempts to disqualify my point of reference they are attempting to disqualify my only proof of existence. That is the reason people fight to the death for their beliefs; without them they feel they would not exist.

A simple way of explaining this is to refer to the eye. Though the eye sees, it does not see itself, cannot perceive itself at all. It can only be conscious of existing by believing that what it sees is real and valid. Any argument that invalidates the images it sees is an argument that the eye does not see and therefore may not exist.

It is the library of our observations that is threatened by our impending death. Without our beliefs, our memories, we would disappear, or so we imagine.

Ego is that part of us which stands guard over our beliefs making sure that we are always "right" and validated in our experience of being. When others do or say things that threaten our beliefs we defend ourselves by labeling them "wrong" and us "right."

Nations of people act as one personality in times of international stress. They fight and die defending communal beliefs. Every war between nations and every war between individuals is easily traceable to conflicting belief systems. Rather than be *wrong* millions of people have become *dead right.*

It requires faith in Nature to open your mind and, hold your beliefs lightly, to use them as tools to serve you rather than living your life to serve them. Just as the sailor allows his islands to disappear below the horizon, we can know those memories will always be there without our having to structure our lives around them exclusively. Rather than confine you to non-existence, that act of letting go frees you to totally experience truth.

Notice on the 360 degree circle (page 37), that any one of the little areas of opinion could be yours. The narrowness of your viewpoint indicates the narrowness of your mind. When you are willing to know that all things are true and that there is no thing that is not true, your faith in the limitless abundance of nature will set you free. You will lose the need to validate your belief system in order to validate your reality. You will know that you are and that your experiencing of and expressing of yourself is all the proof you need of your existence. You will not want your future programmed by the limits of the past any more than you want your child's first two weeks in kindergarten to set precedents that will follow him throughout his years of education.

CHAPTER FIVE

ARAS—An Acronym for Successful Relationships

Acceptance

R

A

S

The first "A" in the word ARAS stands for *acceptance*. When we, the Human Family, do not accept a person his natural tendency is to destroy himself. This is the same process by which forests thin themselves of lesser trees and shrubs to avoid becoming overtangled and overgrown. It is the same process which guides schools of fish to divest themselves of the weaker ones to the predators. This is a natural and beautiful process. It is sometimes called survival of the fittest. (Fittest being defined as able and willing to serve the Family.) There is, however, one major difference between us and the creatures mentioned above. We often do not make our decisions of acceptance or rejection based on whether or not a person is strong or weak or whether he serves our society. We often make our decision of acceptance or rejection based on whether or not the person in question is adept at playing our "social games."

Social games are exciting because they change constantly. I was a teenager during the fifties and attended a giant high school in Southern California. We traded our individuality for acceptance in unique ways. The boys wore pegged Levis with no belt, cuffs rolled inside and worn low enough so when the shirt rode up at least two inches of buttocks were visible. Shirt sleeves were rolled up all the way to the armpits with buttons opened all the way down to the naval, hair was heavily greased and combed with long sweeping strokes into what was reverently called a D.A. (duck's ass), sometimes referred to in more polite company as a "sham."

The expression on one's face was important; it was necessary to look very wise and at the same time completely aloof from that wisdom. Usually that meant the combination of partially raised eyebrows and slackhanging jaw. We probably looked more bewildered than wise.

The final touch was the walk which was affected by bobbing up on your toes with each step while keeping the upper body straight but pitched forward from the waist—somewhat like an orangutan. The code word of the times was, "Cool." I had barely gotten that game mastered before it began to change.

The style and customs of school have changed, but the same intensity of belonging to the peer group and being like them continues, not only in school but in all ages and walks of life. Those who refuse to play the game are often rejected. If you doubt that the game exists in your group take a look at the criticism those on the inside lay on some of the less cool folks around them because of hair, dress, car, home, speech, religion or whatever.

My point is that acceptance or rejection of individuals in our society quite often does not depend on whether or not they are worthwhile to the society as a whole. It is often dependent on whether or not they are adept at playing our social games. Consequently, many solid, worthwhile and beautiful people are being rejected and because of this rejection are destroying themselves right now. This destruction is a form of suicide which may either be literal and immediate or a system of prolonged self punishment by which a person invalidates his own qualities, negates his natural charisma and talent and finally loses his self-confidence and becomes a shadow in the corner. This tragedy costs us as a society and it costs us as individuals. Some of our greatest geniuses are the most sensitive people, and it is these sensitive people who are most easily crushed by the brutality of our social games.

Acceptance does not mean tolerating nor does it mean coping. It means surrendering to and being one with another person, allowing him to be who he is, doing what he is doing. Each person is created completely different from those around him. He brings his own intricate and perfect pattern to our universe. Without his pattern our universe is not complete. If we do not allow him to be himself without our judgmental harassment we will never have the opportunity to experience his natural magnificence. Our rejection will cause him to retreat into himself becoming defensive, hiding his true and vulnerable self from our cruelty. However, when he knows he is accepted unconditionally he relaxes into his own uniqueness and begins making powerful decisive moves in his life.

There is no middle ground between acceptance and rejection. Each person is either expanding a part of himself in confidence and authority, or self destructing as a result of our acceptance or rejection of him right now.

Acceptance is a tool that can be used effectively to reprogram criminals into realizing that their rewards come from serving the Family of Man. The penal system currently used in most areas of the world spends time and money destroying the self-love and self-confidence of prisoners, then expecting them to "stay straight" after being released. A return-to-prison rate of over 60% worldwide seems to prove that the system does not work.

A

Respect

A

S

The "R" in the word ARAS stands for *respect.*

Every human being you see walking around has a secret. This secret which he seldom even admits to himself is that he is an incarnation of God. He knows that the creative inspirations of the world emanate from him. Deep in his soul is a fierce and beautiful pride of self-being. A sure way into the heart of every living person is to show him that you are actively aware of his hidden magnificence. Being actively aware means actively showing respect.

The action that reveals the most respect for another person is listening to his thoughts, to his words, and sometimes stepping beyond words and listening to the song in his soul.

I was rushing through the airport in San Francisco when I noticed a gnarled old man standing head down in the doorway. Humanity flowed around him like fast surf around a solitary rock. I was out the door and ten feet down the sidewalk before reality caught up with me. I stopped myself and walked back.

"Pardon me, sir, can I help you?"

His eyes slowly traveled up to my face. The gray lapels of his suit were streaked with previous meals. The light was absent from his tired eyes.

"I don't know how to get to the other terminal building, and I don't know if they will have coffee or food there."

It was a clear and simple statement. I heard the pride in his voice. I marveled at his calmness. He was no longer a rock in the pushing tide. He was an Ancient One and he was hanging on with determination amidst a world of chaos. I was impressed that the throngs were rushing by this noble oldster without even noticing his beauty. I felt honored to be the one who had finally seen him. I saw him later, after he had finished a sandwich and coffee, and watched his face. I would like to tell you that it was refreshed, renewed. It was unchanged. He is alone not only in that airport but in the world, yet he carries on with a grace and dignity that spoke from beyond his dull gaze and smeared suit; a man described by Kipling as one who, " . . . carries on when all is lost but the will which says go on!"

How many people do we encounter each day like my ancient friend who have climbed every mountain to get to this place? Wouldn't it be great if we could set aside our own ego needs just long enough to acknowledge their greatness?

In India is an ancient wisdom that says: "When the student is ready, the teacher will appear." Communicate with each person with whom you deal as though he were a great teacher sent to you disguised as an earthling. He has a special message for your unfoldment, but you must be ready to see who he is and listen to him.

A

R

Affection

S

The second "A" in the word ARAS stands for *affection*.

Hundreds of years ago Alexander the Great, amidst his philosophical tinkering, decided to prove a point about linguistics. He sent his soldiers out to gather newborn infants from various lands with the directions that each baby come from a different language background. He isolated the infants in one area and charged those who took care of them not to talk in the presence of the babies or to "affect" them in any way except for changing their soiled clothing and feeding them. The caretakers were to remain distant. The object of this experiment was to prove that when infants reach an age where they begin to talk they will talk in their native languages. Unfortunately for the babies Alexander was unable to prove his point. The babies all died. He did, however, unknowingly teach us an important lesson. Infants must be allowed to give and receive affection with others or they will die.

There is a beautiful story told of a foundling home in England run by an order of sisters during the last century. The home had an infant mortality rate of over ninety percent. The sisters had become unhappily, resigned to the distressing situation pointing, as cause, to the fact that the infants had been found on doorsteps and in streets, and it was thereby evident that they had been exposed to countless diseases and deprivations before their arrival which ultimately caused the babies' weakened conditions and early deaths.

As the story goes, a woman who had raised her own family came to work in the orphanage. Her duties were limited to mopping and washing, but her maternal instincts were constantly assaulted by crying babies. When she began to comfort them she was told that the infants were probably going to die anyway, and that with the amount of work to be done there simply was not time for nurturing other than by physical maintenance.

Nevertheless, she obtained permission and while doing her chores spent time cuddling and soothing the tiny folks. To the amazement of everyone except the cleaning lady the babies began to improve. They gained weight and began cooing and playing. The mortality rate changed from 90% to 10% almost overnight. The story has been told so often I no longer remember where I first heard it. Of this I'm certain, the story is a true one and has been enacted in thousands of different situations involving infant mortality.

We are no different than those infants. We must share affection with those in our universe or we will die. Death, as a result of withheld affection may not come as quickly or as mercifully for adults as it does for infants. It is, nevertheless, just as predictable.

A study by Dr. O. Carl Simonton and his wife, Stephanie Mathews-Simonton, who is Program Director of the Cancer Counseling Research Center in Fort Worth, Texas, states that in nearly every case of terminally ill cancer patients there has been the loss of a serious and central love object from six to eighteen months prior to the onset of the disease. Thus, their study gives additional proof that we are not independent of one another, that we are linked and fueled by a common source of energy that inspires our dreams and keeps the technical mechanism of our bodies working perfectly each day.

We pass this "life force" to each other through the means of affection. It is vitally important to your health that you both give affection to others and receive affection from them. True affection is not necessarily exchanged by hugging and kissing. Those acts can be performed without any exchange of affection at all.

Infants are particularly vulnerable not only because they are delicate, but also because they are confined to cribs and cradles and are unable to go to other beings to exchange affection. While their helplessness makes them highly vulnerable that may be the reason they are made to be so irresistible. I can't be near a baby without feeling my heart opening.

Some people find the sharing of love with other human beings so difficult they turn their affections toward animals. These otherwise lonely people fulfill their needs for affection by giving to and receiving from the love objects in their lives—their pets. By doing so, they exchange the same vital life energy that is exchanged between humans. That vital energy that nurtures human beings could not come from any creature alien to or not a part of the same vibratory pattern as humans. Even as our infants are raised on the milk of fellow non-human creatures, so can our spirits be nourished by their affection. We are the same family.

Of the four disciplines in the act of ARAS, *affection* is the most difficult to do regularly. For many of us, experience with other beings has taught us how easily we can be hurt. It sometimes seems safer to be symbolically affectionate and play games of affection than to open our hearts and truly give ourselves. Games of affection, however, can not nurture the deep vital part of us that must exchange love energy with other beings in order to continue on. It requires trust on your part to exchange honest affection with another person. People in our daily lives quite often are strangers—people we may never see again. To be openly affectionate with those people can be a dangerous undertaking.

The most obvious of those dangers is that our actions may be misunderstood for sexual advances. A simple way to avoid this is to be sure that your intention, is not sexual and that your affection is not directed in a sexual way. If, on the other hand, you do have romantic intentions it's best to be honest about it.

Picture for a moment an immature and sensitive young man working behind the counter in a grocery store. A pretty young lady with an exceptionally well proportioned body approaches the counter with a few groceries. The clerk, his eyes filled with her beautiful face and breasts, stammers, grins foolishly and says something about it being a nice day. As he rings up her groceries, he feels her presence cutting into him like a warm wind. By the time he counts out her change, he is convinced that this lovely apparition could fulfill all his life's dreams. He will gladly take her away to a tropical island and love her forever. So, as she swings gracefully away, groceries in hand, he calls weakly after her, "Be sure and come back," hoping that she will somehow read his life plans for her through his trembling voice.

Will she be back? It is doubtful. This young man has just missed two beautiful opportunities: one was to let the girl know honestly and sincerely that he is interested in her; second, to let her know who he is by honestly affecting her with his beauty and his charm.

His sexual fantasy, however, embarrassed him, and his awareness of her as a real person never developed. Sexual advances and the giving of affection are not the same thing. There is a place for both of them and they can be intermingled rather nicely by the person who, first, sees the other as a fellow human being and, second, as an object of sexual desire. Failure to acknowledge this distinction brings confusion and misunderstanding to budding relationships.

The young lady in our story has no idea what is expected of her or how to react to the young man who does not allow himself to be revealed, and who gives nothing of himself to her. He has not affected her and so he has not involved her. She is gone and will never be a part of his life except in fantasy.

Most of us have been in his situation. He was fascinated and enchanted. In fantasy he was already making plans for the future. As he neared the point of contact however, he made up his mind that she would reject him. He accepts her money, eyes cast downward, hands her the change and pushes her groceries toward her, wishing fervently for the right words to say—then he helplessly watches her walk away. You could not convince him no matter how eloquently you pleaded that he has not been rejected. He has indeed been rejected. Rejected by a fantasy person who he was sure lived in the body of that girl. The real girl who stood before him might also have rejected him, but we will never know because she never got the chance. Since much sexual attraction is mutual she might have been going through the same throes of desperation about how to approach him. If so, as she left the counter, and he turned back to his next customer, they were mutually rejected by their own self defeating attitudes.

Do you play this game? Perhaps not only with sexually attractive persons but with persons to whom you are attracted on other levels?

Is it possible that those people whom you have been afraid to approach are in fact open and vulnerable; afraid of being rejected by you?

People when hiding their vulnerability often pretend to be exactly the opposite of the way they really feel. The more frightened they become the more they act out the image behind which they hide.

If you have the courage to assume that the person across from you is only waiting for you to advance with openness and caring, you can take some risks that may prove very beneficial to you.

Why not test the theory? If proven true it could change your life. Make a self-commitment to AFFECT the next three people you meet by openly and sincerely exposing a vulnerable and honest part of yourself. Ask yourself when the next person enters your universe: "What can I say to him to show him I am really seeing him and will allow him to see me?"

The girl in the grocery store might have been sincerely complimented for her physical beauty.

When an old man comes to the checkstand wearing an obviously handmade shirt the cashier has a rare opportunity to openly admire the shirt. Exactly what is said is never very important, but that underlying message which says to the person across from you, "I see you. You can trust me. I sincerely care about you," may be just the affection without which that person may be lost. Try it if you have the courage on the next three people you meet. And expect a miracle!

A

R

A

Support

The "S" in the word ARAS stands for *support*.

No human being is a loner; we are part of a large family without which we each could not exist. Nevertheless, we are still individuals. Like snowflakes, we each have our own perfect and complex pattern, and it is the integration of all individual patterns that makes up the perfect whole. A person can withhold or hide parts of his perfect pattern, but when he does the whole becomes crippled.

What does it take for a person to be whole, to proudly display his pattern of being, his personality, talents and traits? It takes the knowledge beforehand that he will be supported by those he trusts—that he will not be criticized because he is different. It also takes the self-confidence that comes from having accumulated some wins resulting directly from his own action. We are individuals and each of us has a specific job to do. No two people are the same. The only way we can find fulfillment on this planet is to be allowed to do our own work.

When you are not doing your work you often forget what it is. That is when you most need support. Support means supporting others in being themselves and in doing their own work. Each person when he has the courage brings to life a color of light, a component of the whole unlike anything we have ever seen before. There may be some similarities. For instance: many are involved in the automotive industry; some are involved in medicine; thousands are involved in raising children yet each individual is doing his own creation. Thus, a core of reality deeper than the work and otherwise eternally unavailable is manifested. The creation of that reality is rightfully called genius. It lives forever. All who are not following their own instincts in personal creativity, play at other people's work; the same as children play at cowboys and Indians.

It would seem to be dangerous for a person to leave his cowboy and Indian games to do his own work. He learned at a young age that unless he does as the rest of the society does, he may be judged and rejected. However, the real danger is that unless he receives solid support for his individuality, he will begin to chip away at the parts of himself he thinks don't fit with society and in so doing destroy his chance of success. Our fear of expressing individuality is reflected in the conformity of our hair, the way we dress, the cars we drive, places we go for entertainment and the houses we live in. It is also reflected in our speech, in the euphemisms we use and in the jokes we tell. For the insecure, maintaining individuality is a constant battle in the pecking order of our society.

The great advertisers of the world are spending billions of dollars each year to create new trends and new fads for the masses to follow. And we, heavily indoctrinated into imitating each other, follow.

Supporting another person means making it perfect in your mind for him to do whatever he needs to do to fulfill his own destiny—even when his actions seem to contradict your belief about how he "should be."

ARAS

Acceptance, Respect, Affection and Support is a simple outline that you can carry around in your head, and one that if applied by you will change your life completely.

A great deal has been written here about how accepting, respecting, affecting and supporting gives others the freedom, rights and rewards of living their own lives and being who they are. Let us talk about the benefits that come to you, the giver, as a result of ARASing others.

Whatever you do—to others—for others—you do also to and for yourself. It is not possible for you to accept another person without first finding a place of acceptance within yourself. It is not possible for you to respect another person unless you first consider yourself respected and respectable. It is not possible for you to give affection to another person unless you yourself have affection to give. You cannot hope to support another person in his work and in his individuality unless you are aware of your own individuality.

A beautiful truth: It is only possible to give to another person that which we have for ourselves. A poor man cannot lend or give you money. A man who does not own an orchard cannot give you fruit. Unless we have full abundance of ARAS working in our lives we cannot give it to others.

The way to receive the components of ARAS from others is by awakening ARAS in them. If you wish to have total acceptance from others begin accepting others fully and completely. If you wish to have other people's respect begin respecting others as consistently as possible. To have more affection in your life begin today being more affectionate to those around you. Gain support for your individuality and your work by supporting those who seem most in need of support. The act of giving is closely involved with the act of receiving. By freely giving these ARAS gifts to those around you, you automatically receive the rewards of the gifts yourself. The gifting act requires two people to surrender to each other. In that moment, no matter how short lived, the two, giver and receiver, become one.

This may all seem mystical and esoteric, but you will see that it is true. Do it! Avoid the trap of procrastination and start now! Make ARAS a part of your daily life. Write the ARAS concept on a piece of paper and put it in your wallet. Put it on your wall and on your bathroom mirror. Have meetings with your family and with your co-workers. Discuss the importance of ARAS in your dealings with one another and with those outside your group. Make a team effort of changing your relationships with the world. It takes one month to form a habit. Keep the ARAS concept working for you and it will set you free!

CHAPTER 6

Guilt: Condemnation, Dissatisfaction or Disappointment with Self

In the outer reaches of space there is a planet in trouble. Almost every one of the ruling creatures there suffers from a deadly disease. There are so few creatures on this planet not afflicted with the disease that they are of no social importance. The highly contagious disease is passed on by parents to their young and by the diseased masses to one another. When any person begins to heal, the contagion of the group soon has him infected again.

Since the disease has been so widespread for so long, being diseased has become a standard of normalcy. No one really even knows he is diseased. They are all suffering from identical symptoms.

Imagine yourself landing on this planet as a doctor and pathologist and discovering that these creatures are all ill and unaware of it. From your objective viewpoint it is plain that without the disease they would all live full and successful lives as they were originally intended. The problem is how to communicate about the disease to people who do not believe they are diseased? How to convince them to go through a lengthy cure? There is another and even more frustrating problem. Should anyone agree to become healed he will immediately begin to seem strange to those around him, which may mean a loss of his approval status.

This planet in the outer reaches of space is named Earth. The creatures are human beings and the disease is guilt. Guilt is a highly infectious, crippling and ultimately terminal disease and nearly the whole race has it. Like all disease, it can only be cured when sufferers are willing to give up the benefits of it.

"Boy, am I a dummy." "Now what the hell did I do that for?" "God, there I go again." "I can't believe I did anything that stupid." "Why me, Lord?" "I'm not much good at these kinds of, things." "I don't have any talent." "I'm so clumsy," etc. This is guilt talk—some of the outward signs of the disease that festers deep inside.

"Boy, is she a dummy." "Now what the hell did she do that for?" "God, there he goes again." "I can't believe he would do anything so stupid!" "I hope I never see that jerk again!" etc. This is resentment talk which goes hand in hand with guilt. It is the same attitude turned outward. Guilt and resentment are the same disease: (A) Disappointment festering within me about me, (B) Disappointment festering within me about you. When you get so full of self disgust you can't handle it anymore, you simply unload the excess on to others as resentment.

All addictions, no matter what they are—heroin, alcohol, tobacco, sex, food, TV, sleep, exercise—are temporary alleviations for the symptoms of guilt. These addictions serve two purposes: (1) They hide us from the disease, (2) They feed the disease by giving us something else of which to be ashamed. The syndrome is thus perpetuated.

We avoid looking at our guilt because we do not see it as a disease but rather as a fault within ourselves we feel unable to correct. It seems easier to keep the symptoms anesthetized by playing avoidance games than to uncover the pain, only to learn it cannot be cured. In order to recognize that there is a disease let's look at how we would be without the disease.

You came onto this planet pure and perfect and whole. The basic platform of humanity is perfect. Each human being is a perfect part of the whole of existence. The whole of existence is God—God is perfect. Each human being is perfect. To describe ourselves or others as imperfect is blasphemy against the perfect pattern to which we all belong.

There was a time on planet earth when man was very different from what he is now. He roamed freely through the forests and over the plains. His life's work was simply survival. Eventually man evolved and began to form societies, and problems began to arise. Housing, food and defense all had to be arranged by a leader or a group of leaders. Cooperation of the community was necessary, and it was up to these leaders to enforce it. In their primitive minds fear was the only tool they had. They used the threat of death, pain and imprisonment to hold the community under their rule. As society advanced a more efficient method than killing people or putting them in prisons was found to keep them under the will of the leaders. The leaders learned to create inside of the minds of masses personal prisons with personal executioners. Through constant indoctrination the masses became slowly but surely convinced that they were inherently evil, inherently wrong. They eventually believed that when left to their own devices most of what they would do would be wrong or stupid or evil.

After several generations of this teaching it became widely accepted that only with the guidance and the leadership of those in power could individuals lead lives in which there would be success and goodness, lives which would not be destroyed by the perverse natures of themselves and others.

Prior to that mass programming right and wrong merely meant correct versus incorrect or efficient versus inefficient or workable versus unworkable. It was through the advent of religion and government which used guilt as a tool to control the masses that we learned to experience right and wrong as deep, personal and emotional blame. Being right on any matter has come to mean being validated. This is not to say that your actions or your thoughts are validated or invalidated; rather, I am saying that by the personal nature of the right/wrong game, *you* are validated or invalidated.

In simpler terms, we have been told that we cannot be trusted to be exactly who we are. We must be disciplined, watched and policed, otherwise we will not be a society of good upstanding citizens! Most of us feel that because man's nature is weak and dishonest we must have the external controls of police and armies and internal controls of implanted guilt. This has become a self-fulfilling prophecy. Man has lived for so long under reminders of his perverse nature he behaves just as he has been programmed.

We have passed the disease of guilt down through the centuries. We have learned that guilt is a right way to think, a right way to be and a necessary tool in raising children. Many Christian sects unashamedly teach that people are born evil and that only by accepting Jesus Christ as their personal Saviour can they be saved from their own wickedness. Yet, in the scriptures Jesus reminds us continually that *our only sin is guilt* because it separates us from unity with ALL OF LIFE—God.

We are born to fly. We are born to soar on the summer breezes. We are born to play and laugh as children. We are born to create beauty and harmony by weaving delicately balanced patterns with one another; the perfect tapestry of human life on planet Earth. Most of the weavers have lost confidence in themselves and each other. They have lost the ability to see themselves as God persons. Each focuses his attention instead on his weaknesses and inabilities. He covers up the terrible emptiness that comes from hiding his face from God by pretending to be grand; grand clothes, grand cars. He talks and walks just so. He wants people to not see that confusion, loneliness and fear permeate the deep well of his being.

Some non-Christian religions teach that we are only living these lives in order to make restitution for past evils. They have mistaken the meaning of karma. Pseudo-Christian religions teach that God is a revengeful monster. They plant in the minds of their followers assurances that someday God will come and when he does they will be horribly punished for their evil lives.

Parents teaching their children how to play the social game use guilt as a way to destroy or discourage "wrong" actions, i.e., actions that are not understood by parents. We as parents often forget that our children do not come from us but through us. We also forget that, like us, our children have lived forever and are our brothers and sisters and not our property.

From the time a child is born into this life until the time he is old enough to fend for himself, he learns the basic disciplines necessary for social acceptance. Those disciplines may include eating, washing, sanitary bathroom habits and a sense of etiquette around others. Who decided which etiquette is good etiquette? What are good eating habits or good personal hygiene habits? And by what authority other than being larger and in control of guilt buttons does mother, father, school, teacher, priest, preacher or policeman make those decisions? Who gave that policeman or parent the great magic formula of good and bad? If children were left totally on their own to do whatever they want with their lives without learning any of our social skills, would they become non-educated? dirty? unkempt? criminals?

Let's take a look at the other societies inhabiting this planet; the societies of birds, fish and animals. Compared to our human statistics how many of them are criminals? How many are bad? How many of them are dirty? How many have bad sanitary habits, bad personal hygiene and bad eating habits? Do we see anarchy rampaging through the animal world or the world of birds, insects or fish? Or do we see perfect harmonious balance between them all? What then makes us think that teaching children that they are wrong to be their natural selves is saving them from a great evil? The evil is in our minds.

We are taking the perfect flowers of nature and teaching them that something is wrong with them. When a child messes or wets his pants what damage do we do to that child's love for himself when we teach him that his fecal matter or his urine is dirty? We contradict ourselves. When the food goes in the top we say, "Now sit up and eat this. It's yummy and it's good for you." When the same materials come out the bottom we say, "Nasty, icky poo!" So the child learns from the greatest of authorities that anything to do with that part of his body is bad. "Ass," "balls," "cock," "pussy," are nicknames for those body parts and they are classified, "dirty words"; whereas, "noggin," "pinky," "breadbasket," and "peepers," are also nicknames for body parts and are acceptable. Who decides what is good and bad? What deep sexual blocks do we create when we punish or slap children for playing with their genitals? Where did we get the authority or the great, almighty knowledge that playing with one's genitals is somehow wrong or bad? Where in the scriptures do we find Jesus the Christ telling us that children should be slapped for playing with their genitals?

Our society directs that we all have certain social graces, that we use toilets, bathe ourselves, use proper table manners and acceptable language. These can all be taught to children in terms of what works and what doesn't work. We can teach that one type of action produces certain rewards and another type does not. We can use words like correct-incorrect, effective-noneffective instead of emotionally impairing words like right-wrong and good-bad.

Children must sometimes think it strange that dogs, cats, birds, horses, cows and fish all urinate and defecate at will wherever they are and it is not labeled dirty. Why, steer manure is even used to grow our food!

My intention here is not to point out that what we have done in the spreading of the disease called guilt is wrong, but that it is inefficient. You and I have habits that undermine the self confidence and God Consciousness of children who come under our authority. Yet, we are doing the very best we know how to do. Our teaching comes from the deepseated programming of right and wrong under which we have been raised.

Our belief systems have trapped us into certain ways of life that can only be changed by changing those belief systems. In the United States of America we are constantly hiring more policemen and arming them with better weapons. Much of this military might is used to protect our children from each other. Where did they learn that they were that bad? At a high school dance almost anywhere in the US, it is common to see squads of militarily trained "correction officers" wearing guns capable of blowing the engine block of any car to smithereens or of stopping a giant grizzly bear dead in its tracks. They also carry yard-long night sticks with which they have been trained to disable by cracking the bones or skull of a suspect in a matter of seconds.

Many look at those squads of policemen with resentment, and yet that resentment may be unfair for we have formed a society that believes it must be protected from itself by military might, otherwise its own natural tendencies will take over and it will perform criminal acts. We could reverse that belief system in elementary and high school age children by teaching them about their perfection and their beauty.

When a child of fifteen or sixteen feeling good about himself is encountered by a "correction" officer dressed like Darth Vader, his natural reaction is to dislike and feel resentment for the implication that he needs an armed bully watching over him to keep others safe from his wickedness.

There are none of us exempt from the chaotic results of mass guilt, and each of us has the responsibility for eradicating it from our lives and from our society. We must work together with the knowledge future generations can live in a society that fosters and exalts man's personal magnificence rather than a society which doubts and guards them against imaginary wickedness.

As you read these lines, I hope you are looking with an open mind at your own sense of guilt. How did you develop it? How do you nourish it? How do you spread it to others? Extremely guilty people are easily recognized because they are the most judgmental of all people. They frequently attack, accuse and blame others. Their ability to attack is well developed from years of attacking and criticizing themselves.

Did you ever hear someone telling how he became guilty or what he is guilty of? He may say that he is guilty because of marital infidelity or guilty because as a child he stole money, or guilty because of lies or disloyalty to loved ones. Yet, *crimes are usually the result rather than the cause of guilt.* With guilt out of your life you will have eliminated the actions with which you support guilt. Guilt is a disease. All of the chaos in our individual lives results from that disease in us.

Man has free will. Free will means that we are not being programmed or directed by a God or an intelligence other than our own. We develop our own ideas, our own thoughts and go our own way by whichever path we choose. However, we are also open vessels; ones that can be filled by any passing person. As an open vessel, you are vulnerable to the belief system of others.

As a child I listened to adults and believed what I was told by them. After years of listening and believing, my own belief system became set. I reached the "age of reason" and became what is called an adult. From that point on I repeated from my subconscious what I had been taught and pretended they were my own thoughts. Some of those thoughts and teachings felt good and were filled with positive affirmations regarding my magnificence. Some were not.

On my fifteenth birthday I accidentally shot and killed my best friend. Gary and I grew up together, and though we were actually cousins, we felt toward each other as brothers. When we were twelve we performed the ancient Indian custom of cutting our arms and binding them together allowing our bloods to mingle, and we became blood brothers. Our lives from then on centered around our friendship.

The accident happened in the high mountains of New Mexico on our old family place. We had spent the day hunting rabbits with our 22 caliber rifles and had just come down off a high snowy hillside to the creek bottom. I lay down to take a drink where the water burbled through the ice in the middle of the creek, When I stood up Gary handed me his gun, and he lay down to drink. While he was lying on the ice drinking I saw a large crow flying up the creek, no more than ten feet above the ice, straight towards me.

I set Gary's gun down and fired my gun at the crow. My bullet hit him, knocked a feather out, but he was still flying. I pumped another bullet into the chamber and took careful aim. I had the flapping bird in my sights and began pulling the trigger. A head of black, curly hair raised into my sights no more than a foot away. Everything happened in slow motion. I knew before the gun went off that I was going to shoot Gary, yet I could not, in the fraction of a second that seemed eternal, stop the movement of my finger.

The gun fired, the bullet punched through the back of Gary's head and lodged in his right temple. He fell face down on the ice, a geyser of blood spurting from the hole in his head.

For the first moments I refused to look. I faced the rocky wall across the canyon and screamed for God to not let it be so. I knew that miracles were possible and so even knowing what had happened, I prayed desperately, hoping that if I did not look at Gary and affirm the truth it might still be possible for God to wake me up and show me that it was only a dream.

It was not a dream and God did not help me by erasing reality. I stopped the bleeding by pressing my hand on the bullet hole. Actually, I found out later, I only stopped the external bleeding, internal hemorrhaging continued. I gave him artificial respiration, and I screamed in his ear for him to hang on, for him to be brave and not die. Gary had not been baptized and had always wanted to be, so cupping my hands in the stream water I poured it over his bleeding head and said, "I baptize you in the name of the Father and of the Son and of the Holy Ghost." I suppose that in looking back I even thought something miraculous might happen then. But the miraculous thing had already happened. The unbelievable had occurred, and there was no way to get out of it.

Each time I stopped artificial respiration Gary stopped breathing. I realized that unless I continued doing artificial respiration he would die. It was several miles downstream from the bloody ice where Gary lay to the ranch house and help. There was no one in between. I decided to find a large piece of bark to make a sled for Gary and tow him back through the snow. A great idea, but one which lacked understanding of that particular forest, because the types of trees (Ponderosa Pine) surrounding that creek do not grow slabs of bark which will support a body.

On two separate occasions Gary groaned. I wonder now if he was trying to say something. I shot all of our remaining shells, first from Gary's gun and then mine, into the sky, hoping that somewhere someone would hear and recognize it as a distress signal. Halfway through the firing my gun jammed and the signals ended.

I realized as time went on that unless I went for help Gary would surely die. I also knew that leaving him without artificial respiration would ensure his death. I was beside myself trying to decide what to do. Whatever decision I made would be fatal for him. I prayed for guidance and looked for every alternative. At one point I took him by the feet thinking that I could pull him along the ice for a few feet, then stop to quickly resume artificial respiration. I thought that possibly I could work my way far enough downstream to have my calls for help heard at the ranch house.

When I began pulling Gary, his arms and hands dragged above his head, his fingers trailing lifelessly over the ice, hands and fingers that had been a part of me for fourteen years, part of Gary, alive, funny, full of mischief, now trailing forever dead over cold, dead ice.

I removed most of my clothes and covered Gary, crying out to him to hold on telling him I would bring him help. Barefooted—every country boy knows that barefooted you can run twice as fast—I went for help.

At the house a large table had been set for the celebration of joint birthday dinners for me and an uncle. In the dining room was a long table laden with wild turkey, homemade jams, pies and breads. The folks had been waiting for Gary and me to return. Roused by my cries as I came up the driveway two of my uncles came out and seeing me drenched with blood knew there had been a terrible accident. That's when the chaos began. The immediate assumption was that I was hysterical and needed to be calmed before any action could be taken.

Someone was trying to calm me by force feeding me a cup of cocoa. A mattress and blankets were hastily loaded into the station wagon, someone began to warm up the jeep. Still, no one seemed to understand the urgency. They seemed to be in slow motion.

Gary's mom and dad, who throughout my life had been second parents to me, came out onto the covered porch where I was pleading with everyone to hurry. They were clinging to each other when they approached me. When I saw their faces I wished I could be dead. My Aunt Eva broke through the misunderstanding that was growing between me and the other adults. She knew me better than anyone there; she knew I was not hysterical.

"Bob," she said quietly. "We must know. We'd like for you to tell us now." She and my uncle stood watching me quietly, their faces tight with fear.

I remember that as one of the hardest things I have ever done because in the next sentence I had to admit not only to them but to myself whether there was any hope.

Finally I said, "Yes, he's dead."

Gary's mom and dad lost their calmness. The grieving and wailing that is the natural and healthy way of expressing the incredible emotion which they were feeling took over. I will never forget the scene of their grief.

I rode back to the scene of the accident by jeep. I refused to go to where Gary's body lay on the frozen ice. After having declared him dead to his parents I could not tolerate the presence of my mistake. One of the men held a mirror near Gary's mouth and saw a slight fog on the mirror; he was still alive. They loaded him on the mattress in the back of the station wagon and drove the sixty miles to Albuquerque, to the hospital in which I was born fifteen years before, to the day. Gary was dead on arrival.

The reason I have told you this story is to provide a framework to illustrate how guilt demands and receives atonement from us, how we subconsciously bring tragedy into our lives to atone for sins. My guilt programming did not start with the death of Gary. Learning to feel guilty started before I was old enough to talk. My family was devoutly Catholic, and the way of Catholicism was to teach a child to feel guilty. Good Catholics believed that the more guilty a child feels the more he atones for his sins here instead of hell, and the less likely he is to feel pride, supposedly the worst sin of all. I was taught from the time I was old enough to understand that I was a real problem. I wet my pants and the bed and still dirtied my pants long after the other children had learned not to.

The wanderlust that was in me by the time I was three always made the farthest horizon look better than where I was. I ran away from home daily. I loved water. If there was a mud puddle within a quarter of a mile of our home I would discover it and hop right into its middle. The attitude I developed about myself over the years was the one which met with the approval of my superiors—that I would botch up anything I touched. I learned that I did not have the ability or natural talent to do as well as others in almost anything. I never met my father. I was raised by my mother and her family. Through years of Catholic humility with occasional assurances that I was a loser just like my dad, I developed a dislike and mistrust of myself.

I learned the guilt game well. I learned I was a sinner and that my natural instinct led me to be troublesome and in constant trouble. I believed I was dishonest and untrustworthy. I was unworthy of God's love or mine or anyone's.

We Catholics affirmed our unworthiness kneeling and striking our heart with our fist repeating, "Mea culpa, mea culpa, mea maxima culpa," which means, "Through my fault, through my fault, through my most grievous fault."

Most of the prayers and sermons surrounding my religious upbringing constantly reaffirmed that I was a guilty sinner and that there was little chance that I would be saved given my inclinations to keep on sinning.

At the age of thirteen I began masturbating. No one taught me how. It developed naturally like all the rest of my inherent "evil." If there was ever a sin I could commit to totally seal once and for all the door between God and me, that was it. I knew masturbation was wrong because it was sexual and everything sexual was sin unless it was for the sole purpose of producing little Catholics. I was hurting God and Jesus with each one of my dirty acts, yet I could not stop. The more guilt I felt, the more often I masturbated.

I did not see at that time that guilt was a demand for balance. A payment which rebalances an upset in the universe, makes a disrupted situation at-one (the meaning of atonement) again. I did see that the payment demanded of me was pain and what could be more painful than to commit the same sin more often in order to feel even more hated by myself and all other beings that are right and good and decent. I did not, of course, see myself as basically evil. I looked at my evilness as a temporary thing represented by the devil who lurked in my heart. I thought of myself as a pure and decent person and proved it by punishing myself furiously for my transgressions.

Self-hatred was encouraged by the dogma of my religion. I was in cahoots with Satan which only deepened my fanatical obsession with God and religion. My masturbation habit quickly became public knowledge because no sooner did I start than my face broke out in lovely pimples the size and color of raspberries. They were a flag that I wore shouting to anyone who looked, "This kid is a masturbator!"

For most young men and women, the development through puberty comprises the toughest and scariest years of their lives. During these years they need more support, encouragement, love and acknowledgment of their magnificence than at any other time in their lives. Yet, in most cases these are the very years when authority comes down most heavily on them, complicating their natural awkwardness with confidence-destroying doses of dislike and distrust.

By the time of Gary's death, I had already developed mistrust of my morals and good sense. I remember once when I was thirteen and I was hunting rabbits with my grandfather and my uncles in the mountains of New Mexico. I put a loaded 22 rifle in the back of the car. I was quickly reminded that this was just the sort of dangerous and stupid mistake I could always be expected to make. I was crushed. My uncles and grandfather no longer loved me, or so I thought. That memory was recalled instantly when Gary fell bleeding to the ice. I assured myself (as any good person should) that I was the only person in the world who could have made this stupid mistake.

I might have driven myself completely insane with guilt during the years after that but for one seemingly unimportant incident that mediated my need for self punishment. In mid-afternoon a couple of days after the accident I was lying on a bed in my grandparents' house. The phone rang and my grandfather, who did not know I was there, answered it. The person on the other end of the line was the district attorney.

As I listened to him explain the situation to the district attorney I realized with surprise that he harbored absolutely no blame toward me. He admitted he had taught me to hunt and to use a gun, and to my surprise that I was a good, safe hunter. He told the D.A. what had happened was, "just one of those things that sometimes happen."

My grandfather and I seldom discussed anything. I was afraid of him. He was fierce, honest and unafraid of anything. He was my patriarch and my hero. Without his knowing it, that afternoon he gave me the vote of confidence that held me together over the next few years.

Feeling guilt or feeling bad for "mistakes" or "goofups" is the automatic destruction of your self-confidence. Without self-confidence, you commit errors and mistakes in judgment. You become mentally fixed on your sins and commit them over and over. You create your life by intention. Where your intention is is where your attention is. You create your path in the direction you are looking. So look at your magnificence!

The story I have just told you is tragic and sorrowful. Yet, it had a perverse reward for me, a reward which I had never admitted to anyone including myself—that by killing Gary I became the greatest of victims. I could live the rest of my life with the horror of having taken my brother's life; a horror that lets me suffer enough to atone for the sins that make up my burden of guilt.

Guilty people who do not suffer enough to balance the scale of their guilts are constantly suspicious that something is about to go wrong. They are people who fear going out of their houses after dark. They do not take unnecessary risks. They stay very close to themselves. They know if they take risks, i.e., step into the unknown, the

Great Goblin in the sky will arrange things so that a terrible catastrophe will befall them. Once they make a large payment of pain on their guilt debt, they feel temporary freedom—temporary, because guilt is an addiction, and as such requires a lifetime of payments. When a "junkie" is off guilt for awhile his self-identity begins to change to that of a worthy person. Feeling good makes him suspicious. Old alarms go off and a feeling of uneasiness comes over him. Like a beggar in the palace he realizes his masquerade is seen through and flees to the safety of good old pain.

Did I actually shoot Gary so that I could suffer? That is a difficult question to answer. I am sure Gary's death has served me more than any other experience in my life. I have learned from it, used it as a crutch, used it to prove my heroism, used it as penance, and used it as that which sets me apart from other people. If those reeds had already been fulfilled would I have shot Gary? Maybe not. Maybe in that split second when I saw him, knew I was going to shoot him, but had not yet pulled the trigger, I would have stopped. Maybe, and yet there is also Gary's need to be considered. Did he want me to shoot him?

A short while before the accident we were sitting on a snow covered log discussing a boy we knew in school who had killed another boy in a hunting accident. Gary said, "If that ever happens between you and me I want to be the one who is shot. I could never live with the memory of shooting you." Less than an hour later he was dead. Gary and I both created our own realities.

There is only one way to rid yourself of guilt. You must change the programmed tapes in your subconscious mind, and that job requires immense dedication ind perseverance.

When viewed in a positive way I realize the beautiful birthday present I was given on my fifteenth birthday, to be instrumental in releasing my friend and brother to a higher level of consciousness.

I know that unless Gary had been ready to die—that is, to leave this life pattern and move to the next one—he would not have died. He would not have stood up in front of my gun. I realize also that the lessons I lave learned from that incredible afternoon have enlightened me and guided my "life's work." My search or meaning through the years was inspired by my need to know the truth.

In the ensuing years I have been personally involved in many traumatic incidents, some of them even more catastrophic than Gary's death. I have learned one lesson above all others: The great saboteur of life's natural joy is guilt. Most tragedies are created by guilty people so they can become victims and pay more intensely for their guilt. The law of balance demands its due!

Guilt is a disease you and I propagate to those around us. We find vulnerabilities in other people and use subtle guilt barbs to manipulate them.

The other day, I watched a man as he waited for his daughter, a bride-to-be. She was five minutes late for the rehearsal. He was obviously disturbed because she was leaving him and his home for another. He pretended to be the noble father through it all. The subtle ways he triggered her guilt reflexes, which he had programmed for twenty-three years, were amazing to me. His first action when she ran up to him was to look at his watch and frown. The tone of his voice was not quite that of a rejected and wounded child, but the pain was obvious just beneath the surface. Her happy attitude immediately disappeared. She became concerned about pleasing him, and he occupied her attention even when the crowd of excited people gathered. He stood off by himself and was very solemn.

How do you manipulate other people with guilt? What are your favorite guilt games? You will never answer that question honestly until you have made it OK for you to be a person who manipulates others. If you see it as wrong to be a manipulator and wrong to use guilt as a manipulative tool, you will be unable to effect a change. Your manipulative actions will continue. That which you resist, persists. That is what makes guilt difficult to cure. When, however, we are willing to admit that we are guilty and that as guilty persons we carry and spread guilt as a disease, we can begin to heal ourselves.

One interesting aspect of guilt is that it is always in company with resentment. Guilt is not only a disease one catches from someone else, it is a disease one feels the symptoms of only in reaction to someone else. One feels guilt as a result of unfulfilled expectations placed on him by himself and others. When placed by himself these expectations represent viewpoints of people who are or have been of importance to him.

The expectations of God as explained to us by so-called representatives of God are for us to behave in certain ways. When we do not fulfill those expectations, we make God sorrowful and angry, and so incur a guilt debt which triggers a secondary reaction, a feeling of resentment towards God for making us feel guilt. And as the circle goes what could make one feel guiltier than resenting God? So the third reaction is guilt again. The same condition exists with respect to our parents, law enforcers, teachers, preachers, priests, nuns, friends, lovers, spouses, brothers, sisters, children and even the abstract authorities represented by television and newspapers which include presidents, prime ministers, etc. These people, just like parents, have a long index finger which they waggle vigorously at us and tell us that we *should* be different. Whenever you get the word *should*, know that there is guilt coming right behind it! Wherever you find guilt you will find an equal amount of resentment for those involved with its creation.

Now that you are aware of the guilt/resentment partnership, think about people in whom you have programmed guilt and recognize that each one of them has a resentment for you equal to the guilt that stimulated it. What then keeps them from saying, "I resent you for making me feel guilty?" The answer to that is simple. They believe they deserve to feel guilty. That does not, however, take away their resentment toward you for pointing out their obligation to suffer.

I was looking down from an airplane not too long ago at planet earth. As I gazed at the tiny houses, streets and cities, I asked myself, "How can we convert our planet back into a garden so that people can play and do their natural life's work without mistrust and unhappiness? What would it ultimately take to rid us of our crimes against one another? How could we prepare for such a campaign?"

In order to get the answers to those questions I searched carefully for the causes of mistrust, crime and war. I recognized that at the root of each of these was the same old ugly head of guilt, guilty people infecting their society with their own feelings of unworthiness and mistrust. Because of their own dissatisfaction and mistrust of self, people suspect that others are at least as untrustworthy. Nations of guilty people look upon other nations with mistrust. Mistrust of others cannot exist until if finds a rooting place in the garden of your own mind. It is not possible to mistrust another beyond your capacity to mistrust yourself. It is not possible for us as a nation to mistrust the motives of another nation more than we mistrust the motives of our own nation.

Let's think for a moment about two great powers: Russia and China. On the one side, we have a large mass of land in the possession of people who actively mistrust the motives of a people who own the mass of land on the other side.

What is the commonality of the two groups? They are both members of the human family. They both love children and soft-eyed babies. They both grieve when a loved one dies. They both listen to music. They both love to be entertained and enshrine their favorite entertainers. They both have a natural curiosity for things not yet understood. They both want the opportunity to live their lives unmolested. They both love personal freedom. How is it then that one group of people looks at the other group of people as different from themselves? They both believe that if given a chance the others will attack, rape, pillage and overthrow their way of life. They could not possibly imagine another group of people capable of that maliciousness unless they first saw themselves capable of it.

So, in order to protect themselves from the hostilities of "the other side," they arm themselves with weapons and drill continually for the coming holocaust. What holocaust? Here we are sitting on the sidelines watching two vast countries as though it were a tennis match. They are each being told by the leaders that they must be ready to hit the ball back when it comes. Both believe themselves to be the defenders and the others the offenders. Their attentions are both fastened on defending that which is good and right and belonging to them.

Can you see the factor being overlooked by us, the spectators, and by each of them? The only cause either will ever find for attack comes from the paranoia of guilt. Would either attack the other in order to gain control of their natural resources? Each of them is already using all their own resources to support their own population. Capturing another country would only increase the debts and the problems for those in power. There is only one reason for one country to attack another—to prevent the other country from attacking them. Does this all sound a little nuts? That is because it *is* a little nuts and would be a little funny if it weren't so tragic.

This book is being written in the fall of 1980, a year that Americans will long remember as a time of chaos, confusion and mistrust. Within the next six months another American President and the Pope will be shot. The insanity of our age may be characterized by a mutual agreement between President Carter and the premier of the Soviet Union. Their pact is not to fire nuclear missiles at the citizenry at large but rather to confine their nuclear missiles to military targets. The scene of a housewife and children safely watching television-watching the spectacle of her husband's factory or military base being annihilated leaves me cold. Citizens are humans whether it is their job to make bombs or bandaids. Both need the security of knowing their country is being led by those who seek peace and cooperation as world goals.

Ask yourself this simple question: Who wants us? Our country must buy or beg oil to keep it alive. Our abundance of natural resources has never been able to balance our national debt. We have the most aggressive and independent citizens in the world. How would Russia manage this country—especially since many of the citizens are more heavily armed than the military? The number of private guns that have been bought in the last fifteen years for self-defense is phenomenal. For arms salesmen paranoia is a profitable business. All of us know people who have loaded guns at their bedside or under their pillow or in their car. Who are these folks going to shoot? Who is that mysterious somebody that is going to attack and murder them or steal their valuables? We all hear about the raping and the slaughtering of innocents. What we do not read in the newspapers or see on TV is how unlikely it is that any of us would be that victim. Even in places of high population density it is the rare person who becomes the victim of violent crime. If we divide the number of murders, rapes and assaults in one year in a large metropolitan area by that area's population, what we find is that these are uncommon incidents for individual citizens even in high crime rate areas. Yet newspapers, radio and TV newscasts are full of the blood and smoke of violence. What causes us to demand of the news media these tales of horror and sorrow? What is it that fascinates us so about the suffering of others but causes us to fear that same suffering? It is nothing other than our own guilt that causes our paranoia, our defensiveness.

Defensiveness has two bases. One base is that there is something belonging to you not truly yours. A person might, for instance, feel defensive over a piece of property that he has stolen. He defends it because he secretly knows it is not really his and knows it will be taken away.

Secondly, a person can be defensive because his guilt demands loss and pain to balance itself. He feels his guilt and he knows the pain is coming. He suspects his earned punishment is hiding behind every ray of sunshine.

Punishment is the reaction of a guilty authority toward those who remind him of his criminal tendencies. Does punishment actually correct a crime? The obvious answer is no. There has been no dead person resurrected as a result of frying his executioner in an electric chair. There has been no rape victim unraped as a result of sending the rapist to prison.

We tell ourselves that punishing criminals will keep the crime from being done again, yet the crime rate of ex-convicts proves conclusively that punishment not only failed to cure them of their criminal tendencies, it programmed into their subconscious minds they are outcasts, outlaws, wrong, bad, guilty and they are the problem element of an otherwise good society.

Our penal system repeatedly drills these identities into prisoners' heads so by the time they are released from prison their programming is complete. Almost robot-like, they return to society to act according to the identity we have given them. In astonishment and horror we cry, "Why that guy spent fifteen years in prison, and only out three weeks he held up a grocery store!" Are we really surprised? We taught him that that is all he is good for. He has surrendered to the fact that he has an incurable inclination toward wrong doing. He comes out of prison and finds that he cannot get a job because most employers see their own criminal guilt inside of ex-convicts, and their own guilt makes them mistrust others. Any dreams on the ex-convict's part of "going straight" are usually extinguished within the first couple of weeks out of prison.

There is no lack of abundance on the earth. There is plenty of money and plenty of "goods" for everyone who deserves them. There is a certain seminar in which students try to give money away to strangers. It is a shocking experience for them. They find most people don't want money. Most people don't really want to succeed. There is no lack for those who do want money or success. The only cause for failure is a feeling of unworthiness. When opportunity arises unworthy (guilty) persons subconsciously suppress it so that success becomes impossible. Their feeling of guilt is then partly atoned. This person will usually blame other people and unfair situations for having brought about his failures.

Another of the greatest causes of failure is, "If I succeed in this, won't I be in a position where more will be expected of me? Given my doubts about myself, do I want to be in the position where I might make a really big failure? Wouldn't it be easier to just fail now?"

How can you recognize your guilt? How can you tell when you are feeling guilty and your motives are coming from guilt? How can you tell when you success is about to be sabotaged? What can you do about it?

Take this simple test: Have you at any time, ever, disappointed anyone and now wish you had not? Have you ever disappointed yourself and now wish you had not? If so, you are in guilt.

Through reprogramming and restructuring your subconscious mind you may teach yourself that everything you have ever done is pure and perfect. Tell yourself that every single move you have ever made has been an important part of your growth and education. You can look back now and call certain things mistakes, but, in fact, you can not change those things. *They are.* They will always be. The only thing that can be changed now is your attitude.

Consider my dilemma with Gary. My last memory of Gary alive is of his lying face down on the ice, bleeding to death from a wound I personally inflicted on him. I could never have seen the incident in a progressive light without first getting rid of my need to feel bad.

Don't you think it is amazing how guilt creates more guilt? It is a classic syndrome. A guilty person automatically feels a need to atone, a need to suffer and feel bad. Usually he suffers or feels bad by creating chaos and failure in his life. He then feels guilty about the chaos he has created and pays for that by repeating the cycle. At the same time he is in resentment toward almost everyone in sight for being a party to his failures.

What if he were to look back over all those chaotic incidences and see them as perfect steps in his awakening? What if he were to take the failure language out of those experiences and recognize them as wins? Wouldn't he then be able to focus his mind and behold the magnificence of himself rather than creating his imaginary sordidness? By focusing his mind on his magnificence he would begin to reprogram his subconscious and his life toward magnificent accomplishments. The thing that stops us from doing this instantly is our need to be victims which is our purpose for failing.

It takes courage to challenge life knowing there is a chance of failing. It is much easier to pretend to be oppressed to the point where no one will expect you to win, and then no one will blame you when you fail.

The challenge I am offering you is one which provides infinite personal opportunity and one that requires monumental undertaking. At this point in the evolution of man we are recognizing that much of the previous programming of the human mind is contrary to our personal and global goals.

Those who choose can cleanse and reprogram their thinking and evaluating processes in order to enjoy freedom, success and peace throughout their lives. From that point on, each can develop his life with wins and positive affirmations toward real fulfillment.

The light that is the source of life will then lose its muddiness and become clear. We will see ourselves as eternal beings and recognize our place in eternity. Our health will be excellent for we will no longer have a need to suffer. Our illusion of loneliness will disappear, and we will be cradled by the billions of loving people around us. We will recognize death as a birth into the greater life and will gain confidence and peace by releasing the death grip with which guilt has strangled our lives.

Your Life Is Inspired By Your Dreams,
Motivated By Your Fears, and Sabotaged By Your Guilts.

I hope you will begin immediately to erase the saboteur called guilt from your life. The two best ways I know how to cure guilt, which in truth means to reprogram your subconscious mind into seeing your magnificence rather than you illusionary faults, are: (1) The effective administration of positive affirmations (affirmations are covered in chapter 6); and (2) Creating and acknowledging an abundance of wins every day of your life.

Acknowledged wins automatically lead to self-love and guilt cannot exist in the presence of self-love. When you gain the courage to love yourself more each day by winning more each day the hold guilt has on you will lessen each day.

You are at this moment reading a book that was written through me some time ago. I may now be in another life and/or on another planet. Even as you read these words, however, be assured that wherever I am my intention, my dreams and my prayers are that you are now making the decision to eradicate the disease of guilt from your life, and that you are learning to love yourself more every day for the winner that you are. When you and I both make this commitment we will begin to erase this deadly disease from our society. We will no longer manipulate each other through our guilt. Hence, not only guilt, but its ugly brother resentment will begin to disappear. Then maybe, we can save our sanity and restore our planet to the garden which we were originally given.

CHAPTER SEVEN

The Triangle

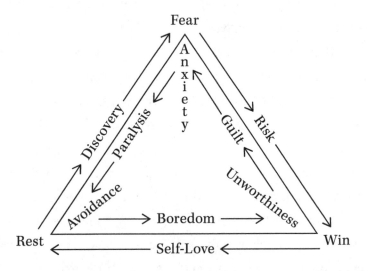

Being in charge of your life means moving from Fear (the positive motivator), through Risk into Win (a place of worthiness and success), through Self-Love into Rest (a place of restoration and reestablishing), and finally through Discovery back into Fear.

Y ou see on this page a triangle. I will use this triangle to show how we either progress or regress in our daily lives. The upper most point is FEAR. The lower right hand point is WIN, and the lower left hand point is REST.

At any given time you are experiencing all of these three and the areas in between them. Follow me and I will show you step-by-step how the triangle forms a perfect pattern for your life.

FEAR at the top of the triangle includes feelings of fright, confusion, nervousness, anticipation, anxiety and suspense. These are emotions we do everything in our power to avoid. Most of us have been taught that they are negative feelings and that something is wrong when they arise. The truth is far simpler; FEAR is our prime motivator. The challenge is to remain detached from the panic that sets in when fear combines with confusion. The discomfort of fear prods you on, tells you to get on with it. Fear releases certain chemicals into your bloodstream which demand that you take action of one sort or another. When the feeling of FEAR comes over us we have two choices: one, face up to the FEAR and take action; or two, attempt to ignore the FEAR and remain inactive. When you decide to face up to the fear, you do so by taking a risk relative to the fear itself.

For instance, if there were an important and overpowering person in your presence who frightens you, you can take a risk relative to your fear, face the person and talk to him. Or you can choose to remain inactive. Results of that decision may be far reaching in your life.. If you decide to risk, you must gather courage you may think you don't have and your growth depends on you doing just that.

One way to gain courage is to tell yourself through positive affirmations that you are bigger than the FEAR and that the magnitude of the risk is always exaggerated by your False Expectations Appearing Real. RISK appears on the outside of the line with arrows showing that RISK leads automatically to WIN, When you take a RISK relative to your FEAR, you always WIN. We will take more about that in a moment.

What if you decide not to take the RISK—to hide and remain securely inactive? The FEAR converts to anxiety and pulls you inside the triangle where there is no action and sends you into paralysis. Paralysis appears on the inside of the triangle going the opposite direction. You can not abolish fear; it cannot be done. You have just decided whether to allow FEAR to motivate you or paralyze you.

Taking the RISK and speaking to that important person automatically made you a winner. Did the person then accept you with open arms? Probably not. It does mean, however, that you moved beyond your fear and by doing so gained an important victory. You have a new sense of yourself, more confidence and self respect and you made new and positive steps in your growth by the act of taking a RISK. You are now able to realize that you are larger than your fears.

In the WIN corner of the triangle you also have two options between which to decide. They are the same options you had regarding FEAR: one is to be positively active—to control and be the creator of your experiences; the other is to remain passive and allow the subconscious habit patterns to lead you. Taking positive action means validating yourself as a winner, admitting you won, championing yourself for the winner that you are and loving yourself. Self-love is the bottom line of all successful human endeavor.

If, however, you decide not to take action and that you are unworthy of being a winner, the unworthiness pulls you inside of the triangle and into guilt. You will then travel back up into anxiety and from anxiety to paralysis and so on. Notice the arrows on the inside of the triangle are going the opposite direction of those on the outside of the triangle. Failing to take positive action with your life causes you to spiral backward along the "victim's path" inside the triangle. The process of your growth and unfoldment is dependent on your having the courage to take positive action. When you do not take positive action you become a victim.

Victims are people who are assaulted by the situations in the world around them. Winners are people who are in charge of their actions and reactions and accountable for results. They may not always get what they go after but they are always winners because they have the courage to make deliberate decisions and commitments.

Along the path of action from WIN validate your win, love yourself for the winner that you are and move automatically into a place of REST. Once again, as at the previous two points you have a decision to make. The options are the same; you will take positive action or you will allow self-doubt and mistrust to influence your mind.

REST as we use it in this triangle means restoration. Restore yourself by playing and relaxing. If you are a creator you will know when to go back into action. As you continue to validate yourself you will eventually reach a place where the new level of self-confidence loses its excitement. It becomes "so what." Your acceptance of self as a champion has reached the limits of your belief system. The subconscious mind will, based on its stored information (memories), disagree with any assertion of magnificence beyond those which you have proven to yourself. When this happens you may choose to go into DISCOVERY which will lead you to self-doubt which leads you to FEAR again. However, FEAR is now on a newer and more exciting level. It will be time to RISK again, to step into an even higher ground of self-awareness and self-confidence. If, on the other hand, you are unwilling to honestly examine yourself, you are pulled from REST to the inside by AVOIDANCE from whence you begin to move backwards into BOREDOM, UNWORTHINESS, GUILT, ANXIETY and PARALYSIS.

If you have a victim complex, and most of us have at least to some degree, you see your life experiences whether beautiful or horrible, being dealt to you by outward forces. Paranoia thrives in this atmosphere for no matter what happens you invariably see it as beyond your control.

If a friend sends you flowers or you break your leg your mental reaction is the same, "*They* did it to me." If you are in your victim dance your reaction will be the same whether it be for flowers or the broken leg—"I don't deserve it."

When you play your own game, lead your own life and make your own decisions, this place of REST (restoration) will be a place in which you can relax and look back over the last events on the triangle, FEAR, RISK, WIN and SELF-LOVE. You can see how you have grown. You have taken two mighty steps. Some things that used to be frightening no longer are. REST means restoring and re-establishing yourself on this new higher ground, realizing the new level of confidence you have achieved for yourself and others.

Your life can constantly expand as you challenge fears or it can continually diminish as you hide from taking the responsibility for your life and its happiness, in which case your life will spiral inward from ANXIETY through PARALYSIS, into AVOIDANCE, through BOREDOM into UNWORTHINESS, and through GUILT back into ANXIETY.

The inside points of ANXIETY, AVOIDANCE and UNWORTHINESS are the reverse counterparts of FEAR, REST, WIN.

This triangle, at first glance, is full of arrows and words and looks like a complicated verbal geometric problem. It is simply a graph showing you either a path that you may travel as you climb upward or a rut into which you may fall as you descend.

Here is an example. Fred did not like his job. Day after day he went to work dreading the monotony and the pressure. Most of all he dreaded the feeling that, while his life was passing him by, he was not accomplishing anything worthwhile. He felt useless and used.

Fred got an idea. "How about starting my own business?" he thought.

Immediately, he began to feel the nudges of FEAR. The more he considered the problems of going into business for himself, the more his FEAR grew. Without warning the moment of decision arrived. The small cafe he had his eye on came up for sale. Fred had to make a decision. The decision would simply be to act or not to act. To face his fears and step boldly forward or to allow his fears to overcome him and slide back into ANXIETY and the downward spiral along the victim's path.

Fred applied for a bank loan, scarcely able to believe he was doing it. He was even more shocked when the loan was approved. So in spite of his co-workers telling him he was nuts and his own tendency to agree with them, Fred launched his new career.

Much of what will happen to Fred from this point on depends on how Fred feels about that initial move.

If he recognizes that mustering up the courage to take the RISK has, in itself, made him a winner he will gain the confidence necessary to go on risking and winning by loving himself and moving into a place of REST. Going into REST does not mean that Fred's going to take a vacation now. It simply means that Fred will stay out of the risking business for a short time, filling his life with projects that are non-threatening and that help establish his new confidence, like painting and redecorating his new cafe, which helps to establish in his own mind that he actually took a risk, won, and is now owner of his dream. The restaurant is his.

How will Fred go out of this *rest*oration period and into DISCOV-ERY? For one thing, he begins to wonder if the standard menu that has been served by this restaurant for years is really suited to the locale and to the clientele. Dare he trust his own mind to make such a decision? Fred has moved into DISCOVERY. Hasn't this cafe made it for years with the same menu? Perhaps, being a newcomer in the restaurant business, he would make a giant mistake by trusting his own intuition. Perhaps he would lose his regular customers. Fred has moved into FEAR. He is not happy with the menu the way it is and yet changing it constitutes a big RISK—perhaps even a bigger risk than buying the restaurant originally. Fred has had the opportunity at each corner of the triangle to move inside to the illusion of safety. I have never known a person who does not occasionally slip inside for a quick downward spiral or two, from anxiety through paralysis to avoidance through boredom to unworthiness into guilt and back into anxiety.

Another dilemma faces Fred; he realizes it may not only be prudent but a bigger risk to continue on with the same menu that has satisfied customers for years. Either way Fred goes, the decision is risky. The important thing is that he make the decision, and then make the decision work.

The sense of well-being and the sense of self-confidence that he will ultimately gain will come about by his making his own decisions and watching them work for him. The difference between making decisions and allowing decisions to just happen quite often is a sense of commitment. Decision making is a fine art that will be discussed in chapter nine.

Using the triangle, apply various challenges that you have met in your life or failed to meet. Catalog the ensuing spiral either upward on the outside or downward on the inside, so you begin to recognize how this simple diagram can predict whether or not you are on the path of WIN or failure. Most importantly, study this until you realize that the person who makes the decisions about how you feel and about how others feel about you is *you*. For failure and WIN are not brought about by external causes but by your deciding to feel good about yourself regardless of external illusions.

CHAPTER EIGHT

Problems, Problems, Problems

We love our problems. The only purpose we have to be present on this planet is to grow through experiencing and expressing ourselves.

In chapter ten we will discuss the negative/positive balance in our lives that separates experiences into negative and positive poles. An important part of making the negative/positive experience cycle work successfully is the dilemma of handling problems. The creating and the solving of problems is the framework upon which we hang the experiences of our lives. It is strange that we have such a distaste for problems, especially since we have no problems except those we create.

Let's look in on an average day in the life of Sally, the junior executive. Sally got up this morning, tired and cranky. Somehow, her left shoe had disappeared from where she left it. She is running late which distresses her because two influential corporate officers are to be present at the early morning meeting which Sally is to conduct.

It is puzzling to Sally that there is such a contrast between her importance at work and her unimportance at home. At work she is respected by her underlings and co-workers. At home no one seems to recognize her true worth.

Sally's left shoe would never have gotten lost at work; and if it had dozens of secretaries would be looking for it. Here at home she has no more status than any of the other people, big and little, all of whom are looking for lost articles and hurrying to get on their way.

In exasperation, Sally decides to wear the brown shoes even though they don't go well with her new suit. There is not time for breakfast, but she does manage a cup of coffee which she dribbles on the only blouse that goes with the suit. She decides to wear it anyway hoping that when it dries the spot won't show. Sally's heart is pumping pure adrenalin when she jumps in her car and notices that the car keys are not there. "Alan!" she screams, pawing the door open totally unconcerned about the neighbors hearing. "Where are the damn car keys?" Alan, still in his house robe, comes down the walk with the car keys.

"Dear, you don't have to get excited," he says soothingly.

Sally looks at him with disgust. How could he be so completely ignorant of the pressure mounting in her? She forces a "thank you," a half smile and scrambles back into the car. She is already twenty minutes late, today of all days! Soon she is sailing along the freeway exactly four miles per hour over the speed limit. After all, she can't afford to be stopped for a speeding ticket now.

Less than a mile from her off ramp Sally's left rear tire picks up a jagged piece of metal. First her left shoe, now her left tire— coincidence? Her car thumps to a halt on the blacktop shoulder. She is near tears. "Why me, Lord?" she gasps. She grabs her briefcase and holds out her thumb, pleading to the roaring river of cars.

Sally finally arrives at the office and hurries to her desk for the sheaf of papers she has prepared for the meeting. But her desk she finds is stacked with papers and records from an outlying office. Her secretary reports that the manager from another branch quit, closed his office and brought all his records here this morning. Sally will have to find a new manager and get that office open today. Heavy with seemingly insurmountable piles of problems and embarrassingly 45 minutes late, Sally goes to her meeting.

Now, let's join Sally at 6 p.m. After recovering her car from the towing garage, paying a fine for leaving it on the freeway plus a tow- ing fee, Sally changes the tire herself, getting tire smudges and grease on her new suit.

When Sally gets home, she makes a drink or rolls a joint or loads a pipe or snorts a little coke. While she's calming down she calls friends for the latest episodes in the HEARTBREAKS OF MY FRIENDS, an ongoing saga being acted out by people in her universe. Then, she may watch her favorite TV show, one that involves frustration and spoiled dreams. Or maybe she will watch football, so that she can experience anticipation, hope, disappointment and occasional joy.

If you study one of your own average days, you will find that from the time you awaken in the morning until the time you drift off to sleep at night your life is a series of problems. Though you allow your- self to be frustrated and irritated by the problems of the day, when on your own after work you will immediately tune into more problems: problems of friends, problems of Notre Dame getting that football across the line, problems epitomized by TV heroes and heroines. And tomorrow morning when you and Sally awaken you will be faced with a brand new set of problems, which you will valiantly tackle and over which you will eventually win.

In order to express and experience yourself fully you continually create opposition against which to test yourself. That opposition manifests itself through problems which, if your attitude were different, would be called challenges. You never have a problem that doesn't ultimately get solved.

To further characterize our love for problems, take a look at the solutions we use. Almost every solution that dissolves a problem creates a new and greater problem. When Sally has trouble paying her car payment she will probably borrow the money plus a little extra from a loan company or bank. Next month, she will not only be faced with a car payment but also the payment on her new loan. If she follows the path of most of us she will probably consolidate all her loans into one package with more interest and lower payments which will free her to begin charging things which she could not have charged last month.

This also applies to relationship difficulties. When the relationships that we are in are not going well, we usually create secondary relationships alongside the first ones. In no time at all, the second relationship is suffering from the same difficulties, in which case we begin to create a third one.

Another common method of dealing with relationship problems is to blow out all the relationships and become a hermit. The problem in the beginning was occasional hurt feelings but the problem solver now has hurt feelings, rejection and loneliness all the time.

The goal is to reach a point of maturity from which we can see the problems are our own creations; that instead of inhibiting progress they are really challenges we have set up for our own growth. We are winners steadily progressing through exciting challenges rather than victims hopelessly wading through a series of unjust afflictions. Adopting this viewpoint can set us free.

At no place is sabotage of yourself as evident as it is in the way you solve your problems. People who are subconsciously punishing themselves for guilt automatically choose solutions that leave them in pain. They do not recognize other alternatives, even when those alternatives are explained to them. Their needs for atonement blot out everything except opportunities to humiliate and punish themselves.

Among solutions which challenge and invigorate us there is always opportunity for self-approval and growth.

CHAPTER NINE

Making Decisions

How many decisions do you make in an average day? Five? Twenty? Is it not true that, in fact, the course of your life from second to second is being decided by you even though such decisions are not always conscious and deliberate? I believe that if you look inside yourself with patience and self-love you will discover that the greatest gift you can give yourself is freedom, release from your own tyranny. Your self-imposed limitation and harassment is echoed by those around you. They intuitively know how you feel about yourself as they watch you making the decisions that set you up for failure and sorrow. Their nature tells them to treat you as you treat yourself. Some people in your universe are no doubt wondering why they feel inclined to treat you with disrespect and why they feel it necessary to withhold affection, not knowing they are following your subconscious directions as to how you want to be treated.

Every one of the thousands of decisions you make gives you an opportunity for self-validation. What percentage of those decisions do you actually make in your favor? Do you make "sacrifice" decisions? These are decisions which place you and your importance on a lesser plane than something else. An example: You have worked hard today and are ready to rest and play, but a friend calls and asks you to help on a difficult yet non-urgent job. What do you do? Vote for yourself or the friend and the non-urgent task? Another example: You are in a conversation with friends and a subject comes up about which you have personal experience. To share that experience would gain you greater respect in their eyes. Are you too embarrassed to speak up? If you do relate your experience, do you make it seem small and unimportant? Do you leave out details that would put you in favorable light? What is your decision? Yet another example: You are in a conversation with friends and a subject comes up. You have an overwhelming urge to dominate the conversation with stories that show you to be the most expert in the subject being discussed. Your domination leaves others feeling as though their contributions were worthless. They resent you for not respecting their experiences. You have created their disrespect out of disrespect for yourself which causes you to "overkill" in your quest for a respect from others that you do not have for yourself. What decision will you make in this situation? Will you vote for yourself? If so, your friends will leave the conversation enlightened by your viewpoint and warmed by your support of theirs.

An excellent way to begin the discovery of yourself and the way you make decisions is to take an ARAS RETREAT. Spend twenty-four hours in complete silence and non-communication. During these twenty-four hours, note in a notebook every time you become aware of making a decision. Note the decision and whether it was deliberate or automatic. Then in parenthesis write a decision that would have better allowed you to express and experience yourself on the highest level possible.

At the end of this twenty-four hours take a couple more silent hours in conscious review of your notebook and your thoughts. You will discover that everything that happens to you is a result of decisions you make and that you always have the opportunity of either loving yourself and setting yourself free or setting up problematic situations that will embarrass and harass you.

The area of decision making I am addressing is almost totally unconscious. You are usually unaware of self-sabotage. Only through quiet and patient examination will you discover the obstacles which you continually set in your own way.

One word of warning: Be careful not to blame yourself or declare yourself stupid when you see how you sabotage your life. Such thinking is furthering the guilt complex that brought about self-denial in the first place. Rather, praise yourself for being honest enough to arrive at this point of objectivity. If you make this retreat as I have outlined it you will see you will love yourself enough to admit truth.

This chapter is about making decisions. It is possible to read it with the hope of finding some practical clues about decision making and be disappointed to find it deals only with deciding to love yourself. If that be the case, then here are a few decision-making tips gleaned from a lifetime of making decisions, at least half of them incorrectly:

1. Don't decide too early. Most decisions make themselves when the time is right.

2. Keep clutter out of decision making. Learn to pull out those thoughts and feelings that have nothing to do with the actual decision or its results.

3 My *Theory of Opposites*: Things that work are the opposite of themselves. Solutions to all problems are 180 degrees in the opposite
   direction from where you are looking. Consider:

   The solution to a runaway brushfire—start another fire and
      let the two burn toward each other.

   The treatment for snake bite is made from snake venom.

   The cure for feeling unloved is to love others more.

   The cure for money worries is to learn how to become cre-
      atively indebted, letting deficit financing make you money.

   Another sure cure for slow cash flow, give more away.

   That's right, give it away. Send a tithe of 10% of every dollar
      that comes your way to the source of your enlightenment
      and unfoldment.

   The cure for a relationship that is in a slump is often found in
      a "leave of absence from the relationship."

Looking for a solution to a problem? Look in the opposite direction of the problem.

4. The best way to make a decision between two directions that
   seem so close as to seem impossible: Flip a coin. Heads means
   you go with decision A; tails, decision B. If the coin comes up tails
   and you think that perhaps you should go "two-out-of-three," the
   answer is obviously not B. If you cannot at this time feel confident
   of A, then neither A or B is the answer. The answer lies in some
   area that is darkened to you. You are hiding in that area from
   yourself for some reason. Overcome this dilemma by breaking the
   problem down into its basic elements; then list all the ways it can
   be solved, no matter how silly some of them may sound.

5. Recognize that the decision you are going to make will cause more problems (challenges) and necessitate more decisions. Create these new challenges with a clear sense of purpose and make them work for you.

CHAPTER TEN

Working Miracles

Everything in the universe has polarity; that is, a negative and a positive pole. Each piece of matter, whether it be an airplane, typewriter or dog biscuit, has an invisible electromagnetic field revolving around it between its poles of positive and negative energy.

Our society teaches us that negative things are to be avoided and positive things are to be accepted. We have learned that some people have "negative" attitudes and some people have "positive" attitudes.

In earlier chapters I stated that our purpose for being alive is to grow by experiencing and expressing ourselves. Experiencing a thing is a way of becoming aware of it. Please take the time now to create a life chart of your life's experiences like the one on the next page, listing items of experience throughout your life as I have here.

Put the ages in the left hand column, the event in the next column and then a rating from one to ten positive or one to ten negative in the

LIFE CHART

AGE	EVENT	RATING:	
		−1 −10	+1 −10
1	Don't Remember	0	0
2	Spanked by Uncle at Party	−7	
3	Easter—Overnight at Aunt Attie's		+7
4	Locked in cellar by Uncle	−10	
5	Train Ride to Albuquerque		+8
6	Broken Arm	−10	
7	Lived on Ranch		+8
8	My Dog Died	−10	
9	New Bicycle		+8

There are thousands more experiences during this time that I don't readily recall. Remembering and charting them as they come back to me will enable me to see the exact points at which I made lifelong decisions about myself and others. It is at each of these points of memory that I can re-decide how to steer my life according to my present goals.

next column. You will then have a readout of the most memorable life experiences from your earliest memory until today.

Now plot those on a graph as seen on page 111, being careful to keep the graph as accurate as possible. When this is finished you will have a valuable tool for assessing your life and the direction it is taking. Like looking back across a snow covered meadow to see whether you are curving left or right or going straight ahead, studying this graph can help keep you from getting lost in confusion about life.

When your graph is completed you will find that your travels from experience to experience have gone back and forth between positive and negative poles. And yet it is the stated ambition of most people to create a life filled only with positive experiences; that is, experi-

POLARITY GRAPH

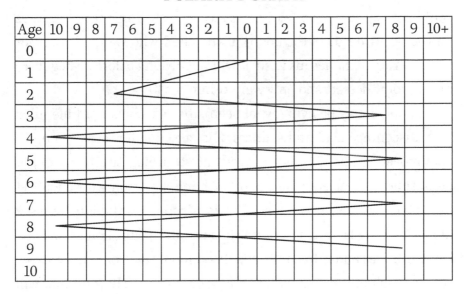

Age	10	9	8	7	6	5	4	3	2	1	0	1	2	3	4	5	6	7	8	9	10+
0																					
1																					
2																					
3																					
4																					
5																					
6																					
7																					
8																					
9																					
10																					

The average peaks on this graph are −9¼ and +8. The center line between them is −1. This person's deteriorating attitude about himself is drifting, his rest zone ("0" line) to the negative side. He is now in sorrow even while resting. By changing his viewpoint he could reverse the direction of his rest zone. He could be in a high state of joy even while in pain.

ences that have no sorrow, remorse, sadness or frustration attached to them. We are like children who would like to have dessert for dinner every day.

It takes both positive and negative polarity for an experience to be real. In the illustration for instance, you see that age nine is rated a positive 8. That was when I got a new bicycle. It was, in fact, not a new bicycle but an old beat up relic that my choir teacher's son had abandoned in her garage years before. It did not even have a seat so my seat was a syrup can that hung over the seat bar. The tires were flat and the paint was shot. What made the experience of that derelict old bike a +8 for me? Well, many of the preceding experiences were on the negative side of the graph. My positive 8 was only possible by comparison. If all my earlier experiences of life had been positive ones, I could not experience the bicycle as a positive 8. It might not even be on the positive side of the board. If the child who wants dessert for dinner every night has his wish, it will not be long before he begins to dislike some dessert and only want others.

A person may be living what seems to us to be a hard life filled with discouragement and sadness. His zero line however has probably moved to the left and things that seem negative to us might be positive to him. And, on the other hand, a person whose wildest dreams come true, who inherits loads of money, has a fantastic sex life with all of his dream partners, has beautiful cars, homes and lavish wardrobes and is free to travel throughout the world, must experience much of his abundance in a negative way. His zero line will begin shifting to the right and some previously positive experiences will now fall on the negative side of the board.

There is only one law that is unbreakable and from that law stem all other just laws and commandments. That universal and unbreakable law is The Law of Balance. When you begin to unbalance, this law immediately rebalances you. For every right there must be a left, for every up a down, etc. Throughout your life, you must experience the same number of positive experiences as negative experiences and vice versa in order to remain balanced. You cannot experience a positive 6 unless you have a negative 6 to compare it to. A +6 is only a +6 by comparison to a −6. Similarly, a −6 is only a negative by comparison to a +6.

When you are down and blue, depressed because the world is not right, you are comparing your situation with another that you have experienced. It is by that comparison that you judge it negative. When things turn around and your world is going right, your judgment of the experience becomes a positive 6 relative to the −6 you experienced.

A child in Biafra suffering from starvation finds a half eaten candy bar beside the road. The bar is covered with ants and dirt. The boy's mother tells him he must eat it. This is a +8 experience for him and he relishes every bite. When this child is at his zero line, his neutral non-experiencing zone, he is in a great deal of pain. He does not notice it however because nature has provided him with this place of rest. By balancing the highest and lowest experiences in his young life he reaches a comfort zone.

The same child moves to L.A., California, and becomes a well-fed and content boy. He finds the same candy bar beside the road, covered with dirt and ants. Again his mother tells him he must eat it. This time the experience is a −8. What has happened? The zero line, neutral zone, has shifted. His condition of normalcy has moved so far into the positive side that the same experience that was a +8 is now a −8.

Trying to rid yourself of negative experiences is as ridiculous as a man going into an auto-parts store and asking for a battery with only positive poles. Such a battery would be useless.

Good News! Even though your life will always be fluctuating between positive and negative, you don't have to feel alone or lost or desolate—ever! You can feel as free, as powerful, as loved and loving during your lows as you do during your highs. The sweet joy of being alive can be as fully present in a child dying of cancer as in a child at Christmas. What is the secret? There are a few of them.

Number one: rid yourself of guilt so you have no subconscious need to sabotage your joy. Your subconscious sense of guilt says that you must pay for all sins, wrongs and mistakes and so becomes the executioner making sure that all negatives and most positives are painful and as punishing as possible. In chapter six, we talked about guilt, where it comes from and how to get rid of it.

Number two: always acknowledge the unbreakable law of balance. The world works according to perfect balance. When I refuse to acknowledge the perfection of the balance within myself and the world around me I lose my place in the harmony of the universe. I become confused and frightened. These are not negative feelings, they are felt on both sides of the graph. They are warning feelings that say to me, "If you intend to stay here in a healthy body and mind you'd better balance your attitude so that it flows with reality."

Many of your negative experiences today are experiences that you would change if you could. You *cannot* change any part of your life until you have accepted it as it is. You are living in the moment of *now*. If you are rejecting your present life situation then your mind is not focused here, but rather where you think you ought to be.

Acceptance is the first word in ARAS. You must be willing to enjoy your life as it is, then you can steer it any way you desire. The acceptance of your life is not the responsibility of others. It is up to you. Others will accept you as perfect only when they see you accepting yourself as perfect. The future begins one second from now—you can guide that future any direction you want by changing your attitude about yourself now.

Jesus of Nazareth said, "Know the truth and the truth will set you free." He also said, "The kingdom of heaven is within you."

The law of balance determines where the center of your chart will be. If you take an average of your positives and negatives you can find the true "0" line or rest area. On my chart the balance would be negative 9¼-positive 8. The true "0" line is at –1. The area in between is called your comfort zone. You have already experienced this area and it feels like something you can handle. Positive experiences that lie outside your comfort zone may be as frightening as negative ones. That is why you so often sabotage your dreams. A guilty conscience demands things not be too easy, that a certain amount of suffering occur each day. We cannot refuse these subconscious demands, for if we do a greater sense of imbalance and thus a greater punishment will ensue.

We have two choices: Challenge belief systems and tear guilt up by its roots, or; allow fear of pain to keep us from expanding our comfort zones.

Comfort zones are either in expansion or contraction at all times. They never stay the same. Some people are so afraid to step beyond the limits of their comfort zone that they allow the walls of their comfort zone to close in around them. It is quite common for such people to isolate themselves in an apartment or house and close off most of the rooms. This contraction of their world goes on until they may be living only in the kitchen. They see so few people, the outside world forgets they exist. When they die they are sometimes discovered only after the smell drives neighbors or police to investigate.

One dear little old lady who was my next-door neighbor in a San Francisco apartment house enacted this exact drama. The tiny woman seemed no bigger than a sparrow. She lived her meager life on soup and tea behind heavily locked doors. In four years she only allowed me to see her four or five times. Her one offering to my world was a sack of cookies against my front door at Christmas time, but she would accept neither thanks nor gifts from me in return. She died and lay undiscovered for several days. Uncashed pension checks and cash totaling thousands of dollars were found hidden in the drawers of her tiny kitchen. It was there she slept and ate. The rest of her apartment was closed off. Her comfort zone had grown so small that it finally swallowed her up.

Expanding your comfort zone is expanding your consciousness. It is from expanding consciousness that you gain the self-confidence to experience and express yourself fully. Most of us like to believe that when things happen on the positive side of the graph it is because we willed it so. But when things happen on the negative side it is because fate or someone did it to us. We are heroes on the positive side and victims on the negative side. Hero and victim are relative terms. Only heroes can be victims, and only victims can be heroes.

When you are willing to be completely accountable for everything that happens to you and acknowledge that you created its happening, whether positive or negative, you will have taken the first giant step toward freedom. In order to make such an admission it will be necessary to realize that negatives are as important as positives to your life. Without negatives, you would be unable to experience or express yourself. You create your own reality. Nowhere is this more obvious than in the setting up of the negative/positive life experiences. When you reach the high end of a positive experience and things are going "too good" you become nervous, turn your life around and head it back toward safer territory. Compared to positive, "safer territory" means heading toward the negative side of the chart. You will continue along that path until you And yourself being uncomfortably negative at which time you will turn your life around and move back toward "safer territory" which is toward more positive experiences. It is in this way that you deliberately set up all your life's experiences. Healthy persons are those who seek the thrill of going a little beyond the edge of their comfort zones each time they reach, its positive or negative perimeter. Their comfort zones and their consciousnesses are expanding continually.

CHAPTER ELEVEN

Your Future is None of Your Business

Better futures are built on better nows. You can make your future better by making today (now) better by ARASing yourself. The *Acceptance, Respect, Affection* and *Support* that you give others will only be available for them to the degree you make it available to you.

The toughest beliefs to get beyond are those that tell us constant joy is not possible. The first step in changing that belief is to recognize that it is a belief and nothing more.

The truth—*what is*—is that you can be happy and filled with joy every moment from now through eternity if you decide to be. There will always be times of sorrow and times of trial for you, but facing those times with a sense of self-love and well-being allows sorrow and trial to become high and exciting points through which you may express and experience yourself.

From the beginnings of our lives we are beset by wants. As children we wanted ice cream and toys, or a ride in the car, or to bounce on daddy's knee or to stay up late. As adults we still have the same wants plus more: cars, money, sexual fulfillment, good looks and other symbols of security and success. If it is true that fulfilling your wants will bring you happiness, what causes you to begin "wanting" again as soon as a previous want is fulfilled? Wants are endless. They are mischievous little tempters that pull your mind away from a sense of well-being and into a sense of longing.

Allow yourself to move beyond the objects of your desire and look instead at the feelings those objects represent. Isn't it true that what you really seek is a sense of happiness and fulfillment? Have you been led to believe that having certain objects or certain situations will bring that sense of joy to you? Yet, if you look back over your life at the millions of wants that have been fulfilled you will see that your sense of personal well-being and your feeling of joy have never come about as a result of objects but have manifested only during times when you have loved and accepted yourself.

What we all want is the fulfillment that comes as a result of receiving and giving acceptance, respect, affection and support and the contentment that comes from knowing that we are eternal. This kind of security and contentment is the basic foundation for happiness and well-being.

Wants are usually goals set by our higher consciousness, the attainment of which brings us closer to itself.

When we seek objects or situations, however, to enable us to experience happiness, we have the cart in front of the horse. Easy accomplishment of goals is only possible when you already possess a sense of power and well-being. Success is not a goal but a tool. Successful people do things successfully; unsuccessful people cannot help but be unsuccessful in their quests.

The universe surrounding you is of your own creation. People and the situations in that universe mirror your feeling about yourself. People with whom you associate represent a few of the many facets of your personality. There are billions of facets with which you have not yet come in contact. You have chosen to associate with these few, however, because they are the facets of you which you are willing to concede exist. Some of the people with whom you associate are themselves going through rough times, finding it difficult to align themselves with truth because of the rocky path of their beliefs, and so are attempting to make the paths of everyone around them equally rocky. Not only have you chosen to relate to that part of him which is uncomfortable to you, there are also billions of other facets of that person available for you when you choose to see them.

Begin today creating a universe that reflects your magnificence. You can re-create the garden around you. The Christ who was Jesus said, "The kingdom of heaven is within you." You have already spent years structuring an identity and a universe that mirrors and validates that identity. The restructuring of that universe may take more time and work than you care to spend unless you remember that this work is the most important work in your lifetime. There is no person or task for which you are more accountable than that of being true to yourself. Once the perfect God-person that you are is realized by you, other tasks you deem important will be simple.

To discover your true identity rely on intuition instead of analysis. Intellectual analyzing is only accurate when dealing with problems for which we want intellectual analysis for results.

Intellect in its analytical mode has as little to do with reality as a battleship has with the desert. Intellect is a temporary facet created by you to enhance your experience and expression of this lifetime. Using that intellect to decide who you are is as senseless as your pet deciding what your name shall be. The true you is not visible to you because the one that wishes to see is the same one that wishes to be seen. Just as your left eyeball will never see itself, you will never see yourself. However, the eye gets a pretty good idea of itself from a mirror. And you can get an increasingly clear idea of who you are by watching that which people reflect back to you. People of the streets say, "What goes around comes around."

Develop your intuition by developing an awareness of your feelings; it is through feelings that you communicate with your higher self. For instance, when you are thinking of someone and the phone rings and there is that very person on the line, know that the person was communicating with you through feelings as they were dialing the phone.

There are times when you "sense" that danger or difficulty would result from one course of action without being able to explain. "Hunch," "sense," and "feeling," are some explanations given for such psychic perception. The next time it happens to you stop immediately to ascertain how you are *feeling* at that moment. By becoming increasingly aware of those feelings you will begin to realize how much of your life is based on your psychic or intuitive perception. It is through the development of that perception that man may finally free himself of ego domination and learn in a way deeper than he ever thought possible the truth about himself as God.

The organization of human lives on this planet is such that we believe ourselves to be students during the years we are going to school, and after the final graduation we become non-students. Allow yourself once again to see yourself as a student. For unless you are a student in this school of life you will not see mistakes as growth processes but as failures. There is a certain amount of humility that comes with being a student which is wonderful to experience because with it comes the freedom of not having to be perfect.

In India all holy people are students. They learn by teaching and teach by learning. They see their own beauty and perfection in one another and recognize they are seeing God. In passing they use a phrase that says, "The God in me is seeing and acknowledging the God in you." They bow their heads in courtesy and say "Namaste."

ABOUT THE AUTHOR

Bob Trask's inborn wisdom and curiosity, through a lifetime of adventures, led him to becoming an international leader of leaders. As a boy in New Mexico, Bob learned from Native elders the old ways of seeing truth. Then he left that path and studied religion. Later as a sea-captain fighting to save his ship and passengers in a deadly hurricane, he watched the artifices of religion blow away in the wind and all that was left to him was the wind, the sea, and the Great Mind of Nature, which he realized was truly the Creator and that it had been with him always. Remembering and surrendering to that consciousness of wind and sea, he joined his mind with the power of the storm to save his vessel and everyone aboard.

Bob then left the sea and began teaching the ways of life that were flowing through him, teaching them to hundreds of thousands in many countries. Bob is currently senior spiritual minister at Unity of Vancouver, British Columbia. He lives nearby in Bellingham, Washington with his wife Mary and their pets.

CPSIA information can be obtained
at www.ICGtesting.com
Printed in the USA
JSHW021213310522
26508JS00008B/16